Find out how simple painting techniques like stenciling, rag rolling, and spattering can transform a room . . . Select the proper lighting to make your home both functional and fabulous . . . Choose the perfect color schemes . . . Identify the *real* finds at antique stores, flea markets, and yard sales . . . Achieve the look that's right for you, whether it's Classic, Modern, Romantic, Country, or Eclectic . . . and spruce up *your* space—from floor to ceiling!

From the author of *Looking Great*—praised by *Newsweek* for its "warmth and lack of pretension" and its "pragmatic" advice—comes a fully illustrated decorating guide that's packed with easy, affordable tips and techniques.

Best of all, the full-color photographs will give you a peek inside Linda Dano's own apartment, to see how she's used these very same ideas to create a home that's beautiful to look at *and* comfortable to live in. It's not just living well—it's *Living Great!*

Famous for her role as Felicia Gallant on NBC's *Another World* and her stint as co-host on the cable talk show *Attitudes*, **Lina Dano** is equally known for her consummate sense of style. In addition to sharing her fashion secrets in her first book, *Looking Great*, she is the owner and operator of Strictly Personal, a New York–based fashion consulting service, and the designer of her own line of accessories, which she sells on QVC. She lives in New York City and Connecticut with her husband, Frank Attardi. **Anne Kyle** coauthored *Looking Great* and is the author of two bridal books and numerous magazine articles. She lives in Westchester County, New York, with her husband and children.

Other Books by Linda Dano and Anne Kyle

Looking Great . . .

A
Perigee Book

Living Great

Style Expert and Television Star Linda Dano Shows You How

to Bring Style Home with Her Easy, Affordable

Decorating Ideas and Techniques

Linda Dano

with Anne Kyle

• *Illustrations by Barbara Griffel* •

A Perigee Book
Published by The Berkley Publishing Group
A division of Penguin Putnam Inc.
375 Hudson Street,
New York, New York 10014

G. P. Putnam's Sons edition: April 1998
First Perigee edition: April 1999

Perigee ISBN: 0-399-52484-3

Published simultaneously in Canada.

The Penguin Putnam Inc. World Wide Web site address is
http://www.penguinputnam.com

The Library of Congress has catalogued the G. P. Putnam's Sons edition as follows

Dano, Linda.
Liging great: style expert and television star Linda Dano shows
you how to bring style home with her easy, affordable decorating
ideas and techniques / by Linda Dano with Anne Kyle.
p.   cm.
ISBN 0-399-14392-0 (acid-free paper)
I. Interior decoration I. Kyle, Anne. II. Title.
NK2115.D23   1998   97-35375 CIP
747–dc21

Printed in the United States of America

10 9 8 7 6 5 4 3 2 1

To my husband, Frank, and our
three beautiful granddaughters, Jenna, Hannah, and Abigail.
Their laughter fills every room with joy and light . . . they are the ultimate accessories in my life.

—LINDA DANO

Jenna with her hand on her chin—and she doesn't even need a face-lift.

Frank and his two girls—do you think he loves them or what?

Hannah in feathers—so like Felicia Gallant! Do you think she might be an actress?

Abigail with her food—look at that joy—an eater like her Grandma.

Hannah & Abigail—it doesn't get any better than this! (Photos from the family album)

To Casey and Mackenzie

—ANNE KYLE

Acknowledgments

For those of you to whom I repeatedly said, "I don't know if I can do this . . ."
I thank you for your patience, friendship, and love . . . my husband, Frank; my
mother; my publicist and my everything else, Vivien Stern; Euclides; Bill and
Elisa; David and Laura; Jeanette; Jill; Caryn; Angela; Barbara; my friends at
Another World; many more friends who would stop and listen; Jonathan Pillot and
Jimmy Vines; and, of course, you, Denise Silvestro—always a believer. And a
special thanks to Anne Kyle—who would have believed we could do it again?
Special thanks to the Home Furnishings Council. Also, I can never forget the
homes that I have loved and the people who lived in them . . . Grandma's house;
my parents' home; Frank's and my first home together; our townhouse in the
city; the treehouse in Africa; the Agars' farmhouse, a fifteenth-century home in
England, where we spent only one night; Winthertur, our Malaysian bungalow;
and the ultimate dream, our eighteenth-century home in Connecticut. They all
inspired the spirit of what a home should be.

—LINDA DANO

I am forever grateful to those who helped me complete this book. My friends
and family have been generous beyond belief with their time and support. Specifically, Ingela Rodriquez (along with Hanna, Petra, Sarah, and Emily) for entertaining my son; Marie Lagadeau for taking care of my daughter; my husband,
Trip, for his love and willingness to make my life easier; and my children for giving up precious time with Mommy.

This book would not have been completed without the insight and guidance of our editor, Denise Silvestro; she is surely a star on the rise. And, of course, Linda Dano's graciousness and sense of humor kept us both sane while straining toward the finish line. I value her intelligence and sense of style; but really, it is our friendship I have come to rely on. Thank you, Linda.

—ANNE KYLE

Contents

Living Great

Introduction

Welcome to my private world. My home. This is the place I always long to be whenever I am away, whether I'm in Brooklyn, New York, or far, far away. It is the place where I feel the safest, the most secure, the most loved. The place where I can pull on my flannel jammies with the safety pin holding the neck together (okay, so I have fashion weaknesses, too), pour a cup of warm tea, and cuddle up in a soft chair. My home is like a second skin; it says "me" more than anything else. I have always tried to make whatever space I had into something of a refuge, a place where I feel good about myself.

Even when I was a kid growing up in North Long Beach, California, when the money was tight and we couldn't afford the kind of bedroom I dreamed of, I was able to find ways to make that room mine. I remember my mother and dad saved to buy me a bedroom set. It was white French Provincial, and although it wasn't the set I really wanted, I loved it. I used pink linens and an off-white rug and I painted the walls pink. Then I added groupings around the room. My dolls all in one corner, pictures in another. I made a lamp shade out of fabric. I made this room my safe place. When I finally moved out of my parents' home, I took this bedroom set with me and changed it to fit a room more in keeping with my older self. I painted the furniture a deep red. I found chairs at flea markets (one I found on the street) and then made slipcovers for them—it was a lot less expensive than having them upholstered. I threw fabric over sheets of plywood to make tables (I still do that; after all, no one sees what's under the fabric). I took what I had and worked with it. I used my mind instead of my money, and you know, I don't think I would have done a better job even if I had had a million dollars to spend.

It's always been important to me to take the things I love and have them around me. It makes me feel warm and fuzzy. That's a good thing, and you should do it, too. Is your son or daughter a budding artist? Collect their master-pieces and group them together on the family room wall. Your impromptu gallery will inspire them and remind you of their progress as they get older. Did you find a prized shell on your honeymoon? Add others to it and group them on a bathroom shelf. Every time you see them you'll be reminded of your romantic moment together. Really, homes should begin with your heart. Your home should make you feel a certain way about yourself. That wonderful feeling of going home again. Bringing little bits of your life in to your home—pieces of rooms you remember, colors you saw at the beach, textures from a fine hotel room—putting it all together your way is really more important than having a "decorated" house.

Very often we go about the business of creating a room because somebody else tells us we should. We buy a Chippendale dining room because it's the grown-up, chic thing to do. But is that you? Decorating, just like dressing, is very personal. Because it's expensive, or can be, it has to last. Your choices have to be really thought out. Maybe the thing that's in fashion today will be gone tomor-row. Decorating does go through fads, just like clothes. Will you love what you buy ten years from now? Think about that before you buy it. Think about your heart when you go to a store. Does that fabric or table or lamp speak to your heart? If yes, buy it. If not, leave it there . . . you'll be amazed at how quickly you forget it.

I guess I could have spent more money on the apartment I live in now, but what really makes this place work are the personal things that are about me and Frank. There are the pictures of our family, the things we've collected on trips, awards we have won. When I look at the awards, they remind me of the work it took to get them. They make me feel good about myself, so I keep them dis-played.

You know, when I look at all the decorating I have done—buying things, making mistakes (lots of mistakes), being driven by what I saw in a magazine, following trends—I can tell you that if you stay with good lines, simplicity, and you take things *slowly* and always ask yourself if a particular item speaks to you, you probably won't go wrong. After you read this book and I share all that I have learned on how to cut corners and save money, transform a room with paint, choose the right window treatments, experiment with lighting . . . and much, much more, I know you'll create a home you will love. But remember, this is hard. It's time consuming. It's frustrating. Take it one step at a time; it's a long process.

I have worked hard to create my home (*homes*, actually—I have been blessed to have two homes, each very different) as a place to relax and spend time with my family. But I want you to know: I am *still* working at it. Decorating a home is an evolutionary process, very much like building a wardrobe. I started with the basics of choosing colors, paint, and carpeting, and then, over the years, have added the accessories like window treatments, special antiques, pillows, etc. It's just like fashion. I started with the frame (the house) and eventually filled in the picture (all the things that make it a home).

I could have spent tons of money (and I did, on the really important things), but the real thrill for me is searching for the perfect vase, creating the most relaxing reading corner, finding the right color antique frame for a beloved print. Again, just like clothes, it's the shopping, the building, that's the most fun and rewarding. Doing it on a budget makes it even more satisfying, because if you ever really do finish—God forbid, what do you do on weekends?—you'll have a home that's truly yours, that comes from your heart, not your pocketbook.

Having owned and decorated a number of homes (and studied design in college), I have learned so many great decorating tricks. Most of them are easy and inexpensive. The best thing is that simple ideas *can* transform a room. When we decided to build a house in Connecticut, Frank and I agreed that we wanted a home with an antique feel—a sense of history. Instead of starting from scratch, we bought two eighteenth-century homes, had them moved to our property and reerected them together as one home. The house needed a lot of work but we wanted to do everything we could to stay true to the period and style of the house. That took some real thinking, but in the end it was really more simple than we first thought. We were overthinking the problems instead of looking at different solutions. One problem was the kitchen. Both Frank and I love to cook (actually I cook and Frank eats . . . okay . . . we both eat), so we wanted a modern kitchen with modern appliances—sort of difficult with this kind of period house. We actually considered paring down and doing without the kitchen items we loved—a dishwasher, a big refrigerator, a cooktop and oven, even real lighting—but then we figured it out. Duh! We installed all of the appliances and then covered them with doors and paneling made from wood leftover from the original houses. When all of the doors are closed, the kitchen looks exactly as it might have in 1720, yet our little appliance gems are right there for everyday use—pretty smart, huh?

Another problem we had after combining the houses was how to get the right aged-plaster look on the walls. If we'd just replastered them they'd have looked brand-new. I knew I couldn't live with that. Not after all the work we had done. We ended up nailing lath (thin, horizontal strips of wood) to the bare studs and then applying thin coats of plaster over it. We let the bumps of the lath show through a little so that the plaster would look worn in spots. This made it look as if it had been there for two hundred years. Again, a simple solution to a complex problem.

I know that your budget is definitely on your mind when you're thinking about decorating your home. It should be. I know mine is. Very few of us can just go out and buy everything we like right now. If you need to watch your dollars carefully, it means only that you must do more research to get what you want for the price you can afford. Style is more about how you put together what you have than about spending the most amount of money. I know plenty of fabulously wealthy people who have fabulously awful taste. Sure, they spend a lot, but so what? I can teach you how to spend the least and have a home that others envy. Everyone will *think* you've spent a fortune, because your home will look spectacular. You'll see, even the little things really count. I can teach you how to transform one room or all of them and make your private place yours. You really don't have to be Martha Stewart to have a beautiful, functional home. This book is filled with ideas *you* can copy. I promise.

Chapter 1

Finding Your Style

B efore we start making over your home, we have to find out a few things about you. First we'll determine what's wrong with the style in your home, then we'll work together to fix it.

I've identified some of the style disorders that I've seen in homes all over the world (and a few that I have myself). You may see yourself in just one or you might see a little bit of your style in a few. I'm not doing this to make you feel bad; I'm doing it because I think it helps to see in writing the things that you *know* you need to fix. Somehow printed words make it seem more real. Once you identify your home's problem areas, you'll see how easy (and inexpensive) they are to fix. You know you need some help, but don't know where to start. So come on, let's get going so we can move on to the fun of creating a special, beautiful home for you.

Pack Rat

WHAT IT LOOKS LIKE: It looks like you haven't thrown anything away in twenty years—and you probably haven't. You have piles of magazines that you someday plan to clip articles from. You have lots of little pieces of bric-a-brac that you've picked up at flea markets or tag sales over the years. You have four sets of silverware piled into a kitchen drawer because you have them and you can't bear to throw them out. In short, you have stuff everywhere. So much junk that it's impossible to decorate or even to live comfortably in your home. You need to shove a pile of old record albums off the sofa just to sit down.

WHAT YOU NEED TO DO: It's pretty obvious, isn't it? You need to get rid of some stuff! You have a hard time letting go of anything. Clothes, photographs, sets of china, bad childhood memories, men. Maybe if you can get your home straightened out your life will follow.

I know you have some great stuff under all those piles; we just have to find it. I have helped you by laying out the step-by-step process of organizing your home in Chapter Three: Cleaning House. Let's start searching!

Junk Collector

WHAT IT LOOKS LIKE: Like the Pack Rat, you have lots of stuff. Sometimes it's even difficult to walk through your house, what with all those random pieces of furniture crowding you. But unlike the Pack Rat, you not only have your old stuff, but everyone else's, too. You accept every piece of furniture ever offered to you, no matter what its condition. Your great aunt is moving to a smaller house and you help her move. The U-Haul makes a stop at your house first to unload all of the furniture she can't fit into her new place. You see a lonely dresser discarded on the sidewalk and heave it into the back of your station wagon. You can't help but rescue all of the world's stray end tables. There may even be some nice pieces in your home, but there are so many different styles that there is no style. Furthermore, some pieces that may be nice are in such bad shape from too many years of use (that red wine stain on the couch really never came all the way out and that deep scratch in the china cabinet shines like a beacon). Be honest, everything looks a little shabby.

WHAT YOU NEED TO DO: You can't stand to see things go to waste, so you just can't say no. Your personality is to be helpful when people offer (or maybe you're a little cheap and can't turn down a freebee, even if it's lime-green), but you just have to learn to say no. If a piece doesn't fit into your overall plan, don't let it in the door. Like a Pack Rat, you have to carefully follow the instructions in Chapter Three: Cleaning House.

For starters, you need to decide on what kind of house you want to live in, and on your style. That will help you determine which pieces to keep and which to try to pawn off on someone else or donate to a charity. For as you know, one person's junk is another's treasure.

Decorator Dependent

WHAT IT LOOKS LIKE: It looks perfect. Everything matches everything else perfectly. You might have torn a page out of a magazine and duplicated it exactly. Nothing can be out of place. If anyone as much as moves a throw pillow you have a fit. Sit on the sofa? Over your dead body; it may leave a dent in the cushion and ruin your perfection. The problem with this style is that it has nothing to do with you. You took someone else's picture of perfection and tried to make it yours. This rarely works because the style has no personality. Plus, you're so insecure about your own taste that you're uncomfortable if anyone moves a thing in your pretty picture.

WHAT YOU NEED TO DO: You can continue to read decorating magazines and tear out treasured pages, but you need to examine them carefully and pick out the things you really like. Rather than exactly duplicate the pictures, learn to have confidence in your own choices. Choose one element from a picture that you like and try to build around it. Even if you are not sure about the result, live with it for a while to see how it feels.

You may really love the way a decorator-perfect room looks, but you have to relax a little. People need to live in houses; they're not museums. If you and your guests can't feel comfortable in a room because everyone is so nervous about messing it up, then the room is not working. Take some precautions (Scotch-Guard all fabrics, provide coasters) and everyone can relax.

Don't Live with Mistakes

When Frank and I were doing our Ridgefield, Connecticut, house, we sent a chair out to be re-upholstered. When it was delivered (eight weeks later) I looked at Frank, Frank looked at me, and we both said, "Oh God, I hate this." A few weeks later, I found the fabric I eventually used, but before I had it put on the chair, I brought it home and laid it on another chair in the room to make sure I really liked it and it worked in the room. I didn't want to make the same mistake I made last time. I used to not fix mistakes, but now I do it right away, because I know it will eat away at me if I don't. ❖

Shopaholic

WHAT IT LOOKS LIKE: It's a jumble. You have a lot of nice stuff but nothing really goes together. There's no style. You might even have too much stuff. Here's what you do: you go to the store or look through a catalog, find something you love and buy, buy, buy. On their own, the things you buy may be spectacular and very good quality. The problem is that you don't have a place for them or they are inappropriate for the room. You might buy a lovely, thick new comforter for the master bedroom. The teal stripes just jumped right out at you. Trouble is that your headboard is covered in a navy blue fabric that matches the navy-and-white-striped curtains. Put the comforter on the bed, and—disaster! You can see right away that it's all wrong. You don't exchange the comforter because it's a hassle and you never get around to buying the perfect pale yellow or white or light-blue comforter.

The shopaholic buys things with no regard to any overall scheme. And you never finish decorating, but you just can't stop buying things.

WHAT YOU NEED TO DO: Envision how you want a room to look, then make a list of the items you need to complete it. Don't run out in a panic and try to find everything on the list right away. If you do, and you can't find it immediately, you'll revert to your past ways and just buy anything. Take your time. The decor of a house evolves over time. If you are patient, you will eventually find all of the things you need.

Now, you may occasionally find something that is so amazing, that you love so much, you have to have it. You can do that, but you have to first decide where you are going to put it (there's nothing wrong with buying something and then putting it in storage until you have the perfect place for it). It may mean that you have to redecorate an entire room to accommodate an Art Deco armoire. That's fine, as long as you have a plan.

Living in the Past

WHAT IT LOOKS LIKE: You bought a house a few years ago and haven't changed a thing. The Harvest Gold linoleum in the kitchen that the original owners put down forty years ago is still there. Boy, is that stuff durable! Except that it's horribly stained and peeling up around the edges.

The living-room walls are covered with that dark brown paneling (it's not even real wood) that was so popular in the seventies (they don't call it the ugly decade for nothing). The room is so dark and, worse, dated. Everyone who walks in *knows* you haven't done a thing.

Because the basics of the house—the walls, the floors—don't look good, you're not tempted to throw out all of your left-over-from-college furniture. *Your* stuff may not be that bad, but the remnants of your husband's bachelor pad are truly atrocious. All of this stuff probably fits right in with the old walls and floors, but let's face it, it looks shabby. You hate it, don't you?

WHAT YOU NEED TO DO: Tear up that linoleum. Now. Look, I know you may not have much in your budget for decorating, but you really can do a lot for a little. If you dream of hardwood floors in your kitchen but can't afford it, tuck that thought away until you can. In the meantime peel up the gunky linoleum and replace it with inexpensive press-and-stick square tiles. This job will only take an afternoon to do and costs less than $100. Once you see how great the kitchen looks after changing only the floor, you may be inspired to paint over the wood paneling in the living room. Sand the paneling lightly first, so the paint will stick, and then roll on two coats of paint (less than $20 per gallon;

Find the Good Stuff

When you are building a wardrobe, you go to the very best stores—even if you don't buy there—to get a feel for top-quality clothes. You need to do the same thing with furniture. Go to the very best stores to learn about quality so you'll know how to spot a prize at a flea market or auction. Learning about style can also help you when you go to less expensive stores to buy reproductions of furniture. You'll be able to spot the details that make a piece look like the real thing. ❖

white is often less than $8). The room will brighten instantly, and it will look like a cozy cottage.

There—in two afternoons you've brought your house to the nineties. Keep going.

Lost in the Dark

WHAT IT LOOKS LIKE: Your home may be beautifully decorated and have buckets of style. However, every time you sit in your coziest chair to read a book, you have to contort your body so that the table lamp shines where you need it to. Maybe you bought a wonderful painting for the living room, but the heavy drapes block the natural sunlight and you have to stand about two inches away from the painting to appreciate its beauty. You're constantly nicking your fingers with a paring knife in the kitchen because the upper cabinets block the track light's glow.

The problem with your home is the lighting. You bought lamps or track lights and put them wherever. Because you've been concentrating on only how the light fixtures look, you haven't thought out practically your lighting needs. Your house looks nice, but it doesn't function.

WHAT YOU NEED TO DO: There are two ways to go here. Hire a lighting consultant (often just a decorator who knows how to properly light a home) or head to the biggest lighting store you can find and spend a lot of time there. First, though, go through your home and decide where you need some more or a different kind of light. A recessed ceiling fixture will help with your living-room reading; a small light that attaches to the top of a picture frame will brighten your artwork; and stick-on-under-the-counter fixtures will solve your cooking problem. These are only a few solutions; there are many more options. Once you've outlined your needs, a consultant or store salesperson will be able to help you. Please, please, come out of the dark!

Color Dense

WHAT IT LOOKS LIKE: It looks like you spilled out a sixty-four-color box of Crayola crayons and left them all over your house. You have color and texture everywhere. I mean everywhere. You have honey oak floors, bird's-eye maple moldings, and dark mahogany furniture. You have pink curtains, red blinds, and yellow window moldings. This wouldn't be so bad, except you have them all in the same room. In other parts of the house you've replaced all the metal drawer pulls with colored ones. You even have a little fuzzy cover on your toilet seat because you can't bear the plain white. If I walked into a house that had this many different colors and textures in it, I'd feel disoriented. It's too distracting and hard to see the style underneath the rainbow.

WHAT YOU NEED TO DO: It can be hard to live with a subtle look. There's always that temptation to add a splash of color—new red pillows, a bright yellow vase—but you get carried away. It's okay. We all get carried away and overdecorate sometimes. But remember that choosing colors for your home is just like choosing colors for your wardrobe. When you are just staring out, you need to choose a basic color (see Chapter 4: The Basics) like white or beige—something soft. And then choose three other colors for the room. Everything you buy has to be in one of those colors or your room will look like a kaleidoscope.

If you love lots of colors and can't live without them, at least try to control the patterns. Too many different patterns—stripes, plaid, floral prints, etc.—in a very colored room look too confusing. Better yet, realize your color dreams by using lots of colors, but using them in different rooms.

So tell me—which are you? A Shopaholic? Decorator Dependent? All of the personalities? Probably. I know I see a little of myself in each description. Not necessarily now, of course, but over the years I have made most of the same style mistakes that you make. Just like you, I have to rein myself in every now and then and get back to focusing on one project at a time, one room at a time. It has taken work for me to pull rooms together and make them work for my lifestyle. Even though I can spend a lot on decorating, that's no fun for me. The thrill is getting the look I want for the least amount of money. Those are the tricks I can teach you.

There's one more thing we must do before we start cleaning out your house to ready it for an infusion of style. We have to find out what kind of style personality you have and what you want your home to look like when you're all finished. You should begin thinking about this now, because it will take awhile to find all of the elements you need to pull a room together. Let's get working. . . .

Chapter 2

Finding Your Personality

No matter how old we are, we all remember the fun of going to the newsstand and picking up *Cosmopolitan* magazine. We'd frantically turn to the page that has the TEST . . . you know . . . the TEST. The one that tells you what type man you should marry, what job you have, or what type fashion look is right for you. What fun those silly tests were. And you know what? Those quizzes did help me learn a lot about myself. Well, here is my test for you and your home and how to find out what style pulls your heartstrings. Are you attracted to jewel tones, black and white, pastels, feminine colors, rich velvety tones, all white? Do you feel best in a showplace, a comfortable and cozy home, something dramatic, or do you like a little of this, a little of that? We're about to find out what suits your personality. Are you ready?

I am going to describe six different categories of style. Hopefully, as you read, one style will jump out at you. Ding, ding ding! That's it! That's me! Of course, what will probably happen is that more than one style will be attractive to you. What does that mean and how do you incorporate all of the ideas to create one home? It probably means that you favor an eclectic look (a little of this and a little of that) and will have to work very hard to pull it off, because this is one of the most difficult styles to create. You'll have a tendency to put too much in your rooms because you like everything. Don't worry, I'll help you edit out the stuff you don't need.

Remember in the introduction I talked about finding what works and speaks to your heart? This is another way to find out what you really love and will help keep you focused when you're out shopping. You'll know who you are and how to keep moving toward your decorating goal.

Classic

THIS KIND OF HOME is traditional. It has a sense of history, timelessness. It's grand in scale. It's formal, with antiques, Oriental rugs, patterned wallpaper, leather books, and old-world prints and paintings. The fabrics are damask and silk and velvet. The fabric patterns may have scenes woven into them in rich, deep colors.

There will probably be a blend of periods, with furniture from the seventeenth century through the nineteenth century. The mood will be old-world. The furniture is formidable; it has staying power, it's not gimmicky. It's a look that has been around for a long time (and worked very well, too).

A Classic dining room may have a Regency dining table and Chippendale chairs. It will have a crystal chandelier, velvet drapes. The molding may be gilded, the china heavily patterned. The colors will be deep reds, greens, browns, and gold. This is a busy home with groupings arranged in every corner.

I'm Not Felicia

Most people are surprised to learn that I have a simple eighteenth-century home in Connecticut that has tiny rooms and very old-world antiques. They think that because I play a glamorous character on *Another World*, I should have an opulent, elegant home to match. But that doesn't jive with who I really am. Donna Stewart, who plays Donna Love on *Another World*, lives in a log cabin. Who would believe Donna Love lives so simply? The point I am making here is that we aren't always as the world perceives us. We have to find our personality and be true to ourselves first. ❖

Modern

A MODERN ROOM is contemporary. It's high-tech, with very straight lines. You'll see a lot of Formica, Corian, leather, chrome, brass, steel, lacquered pieces, polished wood. The colors will be bold: black and white, red, primary blue, and the furniture will be monochromatic. This look has drama, but can also be too cold if you don't add little touches to warm it up. The trick to doing a Modern room is to keep it simple but cozy, like using stark sofas with an Oriental rug. You have to soften it up a bit.

A Modern living room may have a black sofa with white pillows and one red wall. It may have a zebra-striped rug, and high-gloss black ash tables. It's very dramatic. It's a space that can have one strong focal point. The furnishings are simple, but on the wall will be a huge red-and-black painting. This room will have floor-to-ceiling bookcases or built-in cabinets. The window treatments may be just blinds, vertical or horizontal. You might even add a fake fireplace to a modern room. Our first apartment in New York was in a modern high-rise building. Frank built out one wall and centered a dark panel in the middle. We bought a chrome mantel that went above the square and down the sides to create a fireplace. Above it we hung a huge mirror that we made from a piece of beveled glass and framed with a four-inch-wide black frame. It was so wonderful and dramatic. In a Modern home you can even mirror a whole wall; it will triple your space.

This style of decorating actually works well for a family with children because the furniture is durable and there are not lots of little things lying around. And you can use modular furniture and change the grouping of it as your family grows.

Culture Shock

I once attended a dinner party at the home of someone I didn't know (so I can talk about her!). It was the weirdest place. The living room was done in a Country/Southwestern, homey sort of style. All rusts and browns and yellows. Right next to it was an ultra-Modern, high-tech dining room, with a glossy black table, a stainless steel chandelier, a white rug. Going from one room to another was like getting smacked in the face. You can mix styles a little bit from room to room, but you have to tie them together somehow. ❖

Sporty (includes Country and Southwestern)

THIS KIND OF HOME is instantly inviting. It's casual, comfortable and warm. It feels familiar. There's lots of oak and pine, maybe even driftwood you've collected. There's copper and brass. There are overstuffed, mushy sofas and chairs. There are lighter fabrics that look natural. A sporty bedroom will have white or off-white natural cottons (the more you wash them the softer they get). You may have a wicker chair next to your bed. The chair cushion will be made from a handwoven fabric. On your bedside table will be a collection of favorite pictures in all different frames. The bathroom will have a basket of dried flowers on the countertop. Next to the fireplace will be a wicker basket filled with logs.

This is a look that is from the earth. There'll be lots of flowers and baskets, antique quilts, candles, and accessories touching on the whimsical. The colors will be soft yellows and golds, greens, rusts, and blues. This is an informal look, but that doesn't make it easy to pull off. It's not messy, just cozy. Right away you want to sink into a cushy love seat. It will be a dusty-rose muslin. The button-tab curtains will be a plaid of dusty rose, light green, and buttercup yellow. The lamp shades will be stenciled or cutouts in those same colors. The floor may be terra-cotta tile with a natural sisal area rug. You can relax here.

The Southwest look takes in a lot of the above elements, but also includes Stickley and Mission furniture and fabrics in warm, rich colors such as ochre,

burnt orange, yellow, and tan. You might see a Navajo rug hung over a big, cushy sofa. On the table you'll see a basket of twig balls, maybe a cactus garden in a terra-cotta planter. There may be a Country kitchen next to a Southwestern-style living room. The styles go together but are not exactly the same.

Romantic

THIS TYPE OF HOME is very feminine. It may not appeal to a man, but if you live alone and this is what you like, go romantically ahead. If you live with a man, you may be able to convince him to let you do one room this way, maybe the bedroom. You would have a four-poster bed in brass or wrought iron or even

wood. The linens would be soft pastels. Pink and whites, yellows and blues, trimmed with lace. There are lots of pillows to sink into. The beside table would be round with a soft fabric draped over it. Above the bed would be a dried-flower wreath or a collection of straw hats. This room would be exactly like my childhood bedroom.

Furniture in other rooms would be Queen Anne, French Provincial, Chippendale. Very curvy and intricately carved. Fabrics would be light, lacy. They might be chintz and ruffly. There are dried flowers and crystal and silver accessories—things from the past. There are gilded mirrors, like Classical, but on a smaller scale. Tiny, girly furniture all around. And of course, candles everywhere.

Window treatments are light and sheer, but in many layers—billowy almost. Curtains may be tied back with a piece of antique lace. This kind of home feels like a big hug.

Heaven Can Wait

A friend of mine, who has two little children (they're darling, but they're still kids) has tried to pull off an elegant living and dining room. The problem is that the house is small and doesn't have a family room or other large space where her children can play. All their toys are piled in corners in these very elegant rooms. It ruins the whole look. As a matter of fact, you don't really even notice all the good stuff she's done because your eye is drawn to the bad stuff. Now, she can't help that her kids have toys and like to play with them, but maybe she should switch to a Modern or Eclectic look until her kids are grown. ❖

Elegant

AN ELEGANT HOME differs from a Modern one in a few ways, the most obvious being color. Here you'll see a bold, dramatic look but in muted colors. It's simple, stark, and serene, but warm. A living room may have furniture that is covered in all white fabric, with a few pillows in a brown and white animal print. The walls are tan. Prints are surrounded by a white matte and a black frame and hung in a grouping. Window treatments are simple but heavy and monochromatic. Lined floor-length drapes are perfect. There may be a large dramatic mirror over the sofa, framed by two sconces.

While whites and tans are common in an Elegant home, a room done completely in another color can be elegant, too. Years ago I saw a model home that was decorated in an Elegant style and the entire living room was a dark green. Everything, including three walls, was green. The fourth wall was mirrored. In one corner of the room was a black lacquered piano, and there were a few huge palm trees. This room was spectacular. I loved it so much that I modeled my New York living room after it. This is my summer look. It's stark and simple. In the winter I change the slipcovers and the rug so the room looks a little busier.

Elegant can be casual but it's not that kid-friendly. I think of it as very up-scale, very rich, very opulent, in a quiet way.

Eclectic

THIS IS MY FAVORITE look. It's a little of this and a little of that. Most of our homes fall into this category because we grow and change and don't get rid of what we have. That's why an Eclectic style is the most dangerous: it can led us right back into being a Pack Rat if we don't watch it. An Eclectic home is one that breaks all of the rules and combines many styles. That's okay. What you can't do is combine all of the colors. You still have to stick to your basic three (which we'll get to later in the book) even if that means repainting the walls or changing the rug to make your furniture work in that room.

An Eclectic room is like my dining room in New York. The table is Regency and the chairs are Chippendale. Classic right? Then I threw in a burgundy lacquered sideboard. It works because the table and the sideboard are both very simple in design, even though the designs are very different. But it's the colors—the burgundy, the greens, the tans—that tie this room together, not the furniture styles.

In order to make this type of room work, you have to mix and match until you get the mixing and matching right. There's no magic solution to building an Eclectic room. It can be trendy (be careful that you don't jump on a trend that you'll hate in a year), modern, elegant, country, romantic . . . it will probably be some of each. An Eclectic room could be Art Deco (a 1920s spin-off from modern). It could be all animal prints. It could be any period or all periods. You may change it every six months. That's what eclectic is.

Now, all of us have some of this look, because we do have stuff we can't possibly get rid of—it costs too much to replace or it's from your husband's family—stuff that doesn't really go with anything else, but you really can't afford a new couch and you need somewhere to sit. Or it took you three years of saving, but you finally got the Mission bed you've wanted. Unfortunately, it's going to take you five more years to afford the rest of the bedroom set. Until then you have to make do with what you have. So without trying you have Eclectic. But putting a bunch of different looks together requires good taste. That's what makes it work. It's hard. It takes practice. It takes study. You really have to know what you're doing to create a beautiful Eclectic home. If you're not sure (and one day you will be) go with another, safer look. The look that is your personality. Your favorite style. It will give you the discipline you need now. Later, we can do anything we want.

So, how did you do? Did one style jump out at you? Once you know which style you love, learn as much about it as you can. Go to furniture stores that carry what you like and ask questions. Lots of them. If you see a great Southwestern living room, ask if they also have a dining room to match. You may not buy it, but you may glean a few ideas you can use for free. Go to the library and look up your chosen style. There may be pieces of furniture (small tables, light fixtures) that you didn't even know existed. Learn, learn learn. The more you know, the more fun it will become. And you can start to concentrate on what you like and how you'll build your room . . . one step at a time.

Chapter 3

Cleaning House

Before we can even begin to bring style to your home we have to clean, organize, and store what you already own. This will be the hardest part of your home's transformation and the time when you have to make some tough decisions about what to get rid of and what to save. If you read *Looking Great* . . . (and you followed it's instructions), you're one step ahead of the game because your closets should already be organized. If you haven't, you'll have to start the organizing process by going through all of your clothes, coats, and shoes and putting them in their place. The reason you should do this first is because you may discover that, with a little work, you can gain more room in your closets for other things. If you keep your jewelry in the bathroom, for instance, you can unclutter your bathroom by making space for it in your bedroom closet. If you have too many winter coats and gloves and boots and snowsuits crammed into your hall closet, a little reorganizing may yield room for the vacuum cleaner and broom. That will clear out the kitchen closet, where you used to keep those items, and give you more space to store small appliances out of sight until you need them. See what I mean? Okay, so take a day to tackle your clothes and then read on. See you soon!

Taking the Tour

TO BEGIN THE PROCESS of cleaning house you have to pretend you don't live there and are taking a tour. Get a pad of paper and a pen, walk into each room, and examine everything in it. Now is when you are going to make your first decisions about the type of style you want in your home. Be ruthless. Hate that lumpy old couch but are afraid to toss it because your grandmother gave it to you? Remember, this is your home, not hers, and you have a right to design it to your tastes. She'll get over it.

Start by listing the big pieces of furniture in the room. The sofa, the side chair, the tables, anything that qualifies as furniture. Write down whether you are going to keep each piece, move it to another room (you'll probably do some juggling along the way), or get rid of it (and how). Use the chart below as an example:

Living Room	Keep	Move/Where	Remove/Where
BLUE SOFA	+		
BLUE/WHITE LOVE SEAT		+/Family Room	
SQUARE COFFEE TABLE	+		
WICKER END TABLES			+/Garage Sale
FLOOR LAMP			+/Garage Sale
TABLE LAMPS	+		
TV STAND		+/Family Room	
TV		+/Family Room	

Next make a list of all the other things in the room. Pictures on the walls, framed photos on the end tables, candlesticks, pillows, throws, drapes, blinds, collections, bric-a-brac, etc. Decide which things are eventually going to be removed from that room (but don't remove them yet; wait until you've examined the whole house). Make the same kind of chart as you did for the furniture, paying particular attention to where these accessories will end up. When it comes time to start working on that room, you can grab your list and easily decide where each item is going.

While you are in each room, jot down notes about what you would like to use that room for and vague ideas about how you would like it to look. Your formal living room may look like you want it to, but your family insists on using it as a daily gathering place and as a TV room. Toys get left behind, food and drinks are constantly being spilled on the upholstery and carpet, and the room never really looks pulled together. As much as you desire a formal, decorator-perfect living room, you may have to give in to your family's natural inclination to gather there, and instead design the room to fit everyone's needs. You'll have your perfect room someday; you may just have to wait a few years.

After you've gone through every room—including the bathrooms—sit down with your lists again and see if they all fit together. You may want to move the blue-and-white love seat to the family room, but you haven't decided what to do with the modular sofa that's in there now. Make these decisions now.

Get a grip on "stuff." By this I mean all the little things that are cluttering up your house. The calculator in the family room, the stapler in the kitchen, the box of paper clips in the end table drawer. All of the above items should be in one place. It may be that you need to dedicate a corner of the family room to a home-office area. Since we are not ready to redecorate your home yet, you can put all similar items in a labeled box and put that box in the room it will ultimately belong in.

Do you have collections of things? You need to organize them and decide if you are going to display them or store them. I have a friend who has a lovely collection of about forty tiny crystal animals from all over the world. She used to keep them all over the house. It was a shame because they were always dusty and no one ever saw the collection together. She ended up buying a glassed-in display shelf which all the animals fit in, and hanging it on the dining-room wall. Since wall space doesn't infringe on the room (I love hanging things on walls—hats, scarves, little knickknacks) it's like free space. Now no one ever walks into the room without commenting on the animals. My friend took a problem and turned it into art.

One more thing: Go through all the boxes in the attic and basement and stuffed into the back of closets. See what's in them. If you moved into the house two years ago and still haven't opened the box of old college textbooks, chances are you don't need them (and if you do want to keep them, decide now on which room you are going to buy or build bookcases for). Designate a section of your basement or garage for things that you are going to get rid of either through donation or a monster tag sale (believe me, you can make a good chunk of change by selling things you don't need. Probably enough to buy a new piece of furniture.)

Cleaning Out

NOW THAT YOU'VE SEEN everything you own, it's time to start removing the items that you don't want. It will be easier to paint and install flooring with all the little things out of the way anyway, so you may as well start now. The bigger items—couches, tables—and things you need to live—lamps, blinds—you will want to keep until you can replace them (there are tons of tricks in later chapters to transform them until you can afford new).

Get some boxes and a marker for labeling and start packing up. Make boxes of things for your tag sale and move them to the basement. Make boxes of things that you want to save forever but may not want to display now. Put those boxes in the attic or storage. Pack boxes of things that you are going to move to another room and place boxes in those rooms.

Get a handle on papers, junk mail, school notices, all those annoying tidbits that are lying all over the house. Decide on one place where you are going to keep them all. Successful executives have a plan for keeping clutter under control, and you can use it, too. The rule is to not touch any piece of paper more than once. When the mail comes, stand over the recycling bin and toss all junk mail that you will never read. Have a place where you immediately put catalogs (throwing out last season's and replacing with the new one), bills, and things you have to respond to. If you get a notice from school to have your son bring something for show-and-tell tomorrow, immediately help him select something and put it in his book bag, and then toss the notice. You may say, "How will I have the time to do this right away?" Once you try it, you'll keep doing it. You'll see how it reduces clutter (mental clutter, also, because you won't have to remember where everything is) and saves time later, so you'll stick with it.

Scrubbing Up

NOW THAT ALL the clutter is removed and you can see everything you have left, it's time to really clean your house. I mean really clean. Gather all of your cleaners, spot removers, and sponges and begin with the furniture. Dust and polish all wood on furniture and do your best to remove stains from upholstered items. Wash or dry-clean all slipcovers. For really tough stains, you have to make a choice: Can I live with the stain because I don't want to risk further damaging the fabric, or can I be aggressive because if the stain doesn't come out, I will either use a slipcover or toss this piece? If you want to try to save the fabric and can't remove the stain on your own, cut a small piece of fabric from the underside (you can also just take a whole cushion if they're removable) and take it to a dry cleaner or furniture store for advice. If you want to work on it yourself, use a liberal dose of water to fully saturate the stain and then blot (don't rub!) the area. If that doesn't work, move on to a stain remover made for fabric. Since you don't care if you save this piece, you can really work on that stain, scrubbing and using stronger cleaner.

Mix a big bucket of soapy water and wash the walls and baseboards with a large sponge. You'll have to do this before you paint and paper anyway, and it's easier if you do it all at once, because then you won't have to keep getting all the cleaning supplies out. It will also give you a chance to closely examine everything. Do you need to fill old picture hook holes before you repaint? Also wash all blinds and windows now. If that's a project you can't stand, there are plenty of cleaning services that will do it for you. An average house with about thirty windows will cost between $100 to $200 for both the inside and out. Check the Yellow Pages for names of companies.

Take your bucket of soapy water into the kitchen and wash all cabinets, inside and out. This will also give you a chance to reorganize cabinets and line them with paper if needed. Do the same in bathrooms.

Last, vacuum and shampoo all carpets that you plan on keeping. If you plan to use a lot of carpet in your home, I recommend buying a carpet shampooer. The new ones are as easy to use as a vacuum cleaner and cost less than $200. (The ones you can rent are cumbersome and complicated to use, and you will save money in the long run by buying). They're amazing. You won't believe how satisfying it is to have fresh, clean carpets all the time. Shampooers suck out dirt you didn't even know you had and are great for cleaning up spills as they happen.

One of the things you'll notice while you are tackling this huge project is what your family's traffic and spill patterns are. You'll see where the real living takes place in your home, and this will help you decide how you will redecorate. If your husband always eats in one chair in the living room, it doesn't make sense to cover it in silk (unless you want to spend hours cleaning it or begging him not to eat there). If your kids always throw their shoes and other junk right next to the front door, maybe a coat rack and nice wooden trunk will at least help keep it organized. Think this stuff through before making any decisions. You'll be happier in the long run.

There—you did it. The hard part is over and the fun about to begin. If you plan things right, you'll never have to do this again. And that alone makes it worth doing right!

Chapter 4

The Basics

O kay . . . now is the time to buy every interior design and decorating magazine. Look through full-color coffee-table tomes at the library and collect fabric and paint samples, even ones that are maybes. You're starting your search for what you want your home to look like: Classic, Modern, Sporty, Romantic, Elegant, or Eclectic. Eventually, you'll organize all of your ideas and pare them down to what will then become a plan for you and your home. You may have a one-year plan . . . or you may have a ten-year plan. It doesn't matter; you still have to have a vision of what the final result will be.

Think now about the physical structure of your house. What does that mean? Ask yourself if there are things about your house that you want to change. Any major changes have to be thought out now, before you begin to decorate. Think about what you use the rooms for. Think about how your family is going to change and grow. Do you need to completely rearrange the flow? If money were not an object, how would you really want your house to look? Would you replace all the windows? Add a fireplace? An extra bathroom? Maybe down the road you will need to add a whole new room. What you need to find out at the end of all of these questions is: Does your home work for you? If not, now is the time to figure out if it is worth making major changes or if you should live in the house the way it is with a plan to eventually move to another house that works better for you and your family. Let's say you would like to stay put and will make some changes. I strongly suggest hiring an architect to draw a set of plans that will account for all of your needs. That doesn't mean you have to bring in the wrecking crew tomorrow, but it will give you a plan to work from—for today and for five years from now. The architect's fee will be well worth the investment, because it will save you from making costly mistakes. For example, if you are eventually going to add that family room off the kitchen, it doesn't make sense to replace that wall's windows now, even if you are replacing all the others in the house. Your master plan will keep you on track all the way through the renovation and decoration of your home. Make a plan, and you will not be overwhelmed.

As you leaf through decorating magazines, tear out the pages that you like and file them in a multi-folder notebook (remember also to cut out the page of resources in the back of the magazine for clues on where to buy the items you like). Do the same with paint samples (free in hardware stores) and fabric swatches (ask salespeople to cut off a little piece for you to take home). Pull out all your samples, gather your family around, and start making basic choices. This is really the fun part—finding out what you like and what everyone's dreams are. Take the samples from room to room so you can see how they'll look in the lighting of each room. If you're like most of us, you'll see that the same colors and themes keep popping up over and over again. Eventually, your favorites will bubble up to the top. All of a sudden you will feel secure about your choices.

Take a piece of cardboard and tape or staple the paint colors, fabric, and pictures of the furniture you dream of having for each room (this is invaluable when it finally comes time to shop). These may not be the final choices, because as you read on in this chapter you will see that there are some rules that you need to follow to assure success, but *this* is where you'll start. File your sample boards away for now and read through the rules for the basics. We'll pull them out again at the end of this chapter and make the necessary changes. These sample boards and your list of what you need to buy will be your best friends when it comes time to pull everything together . . . and the salespeople you deal with will be impressed that you are so organized.

What Are the Basics?

AS YOU KNOW from *Looking Great . . .*, the basics in fashion are the colors and styles that take you through every season and occasion. They are the backdrop for the clothes and the accessories you choose to express your personal style. Well, the basics for home decorating are not that much different. As a matter of fact, most of the same rules apply. When I talk about basics, I'm not talking about being bland and having everything done in beige (although that is fine if that's your style. Designers like Calvin Klein have earned millions designing clothes in muted shades). What I am trying to get you to accomplish is to create a base of colors and textures that you can build on. After you acquire the basics, you could leave your home exactly as it is or you could go on (and I hope you do) and make it sing with your personality. You are about to turn a house into a home. . . . How exciting!

Because a house has many rooms (whereas you have only one body) you need to plan different basics for each room, but let's start with colors so that you know what you're working with. For each room, you have to choose three colors, no more. I don't care what they are, but only three. In my living room in New York I chose red, tan, and olive green as my basic three (so you can see, we're definitely not talking beige here). Since my dining room is close by, the two rooms had to have something to tie them together. I used the same three colors (but the green is more of a sage color) but in different places. In the living room the walls are red; in the dining room they are sage green. My couches and chairs are reds and greens; my dining table and chairs are a dark reddish wood; and the sideboard is a deep brown-red. It works because the colors complement each other, but still the rooms are very different looking.

Limiting your choices to three colors in the beginning keeps it simple and allows you to introduce the fun things that bring out your personal style. You can also add variations or shades of the same colors. A blue in your sofa fabric doesn't have to exactly match the blue in your curtains. As you choose your basics, you can play around with fabrics and textures for added interest.

Here's what you need in place for the basics:

All-White (or Off-White) Is Okay

When people have white walls and white carpets or tile, they immediately feel that they have to jazz up the room with other colors. The all-white room is very hard to pull off, but when you do, boy, is it elegant. Obviously, it won't work for you if you have kids or dogs that track in dirt (unless it's a room that's off limits, like your bedroom), but don't make the mistake of starting with white and then going wild with color. The room will never look right, and you'll probably keep adding color and making it worse because you don't know what's wrong. If you like white, *really* like it, keep your vision on track by remembering that I said it's okay to have an all-white room . . . no other colors allowed. ❖

The Living Room

Paint: walls and trim, or wallpaper

Since this will probably be the first room you, and others, see when you walk in your front door, spend a lot of time deciding on your wall colors and patterns. I know you'll want to choose white or off-white because they're safe, but take a chance and look at samples of yellows, reds, and greens. You'll be surprised by how much style a little color on your walls can add.

Couch

Decide now if you need a sleeper for guests (it's about $150 more costly), or plan slipcovers (if so, choose a couch with fewer pillows to cut costs). How will you use this couch? Every day or for entertaining only? The answers to these questions will determine how durable the fabric should be.

Love seat, side chairs, or second couch

How many depends on the size of the room. Upholstered or wood (or a mix of the two)? Again, think about who will be using them. If you're working with furniture you already own, think about reupholstery or refinishing now.

Tables

Think about all the uses for the room. If you have small children, you may have to be wary of tables with sharp corners or glass. If that's what you have or what you want to buy, you'll have to arrange them in places where they won't create a hazard. How many you have depends on your taste, but for function's sake you should have tables to hold lamps and drinks near places where people sit.

Flooring

Wood floors, area rugs, or wall-to-wall carpeting? One color or a few? If you plan to use the flooring already in place, the color will have to be one of the three you chose (unless you have wood floors, which go with every color).

Window treatments

We'll get more elaborate in the chapter covering window treatments, but now is the time to decide what you want for the room. Simple curtains or drapes with stylized rods and drawbacks, or complicated balloon shades with simple rods? Maybe shutters? Maybe *no* window treatments.

Lighting

We'll be more specific in the chapter on lighting, but for now you have to see, so either use the lamps you have (you can change the shades) or . . . I was going to say if you know what you want, buy it now, but that's not right. Lighting is truly an accessory and you have to get it right or the room will look all wrong. Use a flashlight if you have to, but don't buy new lighting until the room is almost done.

The Dining Room

Paint: walls and trim, or wallpaper

If you choose paint only for the dining room, you can afford to play around with colors and repaint (it's not that much money) if necessary. But if you choose wallpaper, you are going to have to spend more time selecting this basic because it is difficult and expensive to redo. See Chapter Seven for wallpaper ideas.

Table and chairs

The size of the room will dictate the size of the table (you can always buy one with leaves and add them for company). Wood, glass, or laminate? Upholstered chairs or wood? It's your choice. There are a million of them. Don't worry, we'll talk about it.

China cabinet

This does not have to be a "real" china cabinet. It can be an antique bookcase with glass doors, a series of shelves, or anything you want to use to hold china and the items you use in the dining room. I hesitate to call this a basic because you don't really need it (if you have a closet that you can outfit with shelves, it can take the place of a china cabinet), but it's nice to keep everything organized. I fear that if you don't have such a special place, you'll keep things all over and ruin all the hard work you did organizing the house.

It Can Take Years

It can take years or even a lifetime to decorate a house. It's an evolution. Don't feel pressured to get all your basics in place this week. In one of my first apartments, I never had proper end tables. Instead, what I did was drape old wood with fabric. What difference did it make that they were just pieces of plywood? No one ever saw them. They only saw the nice fabric on top. So don't rush. Take your time, eat off of a card table if you must, but don't buy the first dining-room set you see just because you feel you have to move along. Enjoy the ride. ❖

Flooring

Hardwood floors (including a painted floor design) or an area rug are the only real choices for a dining room. In a room where food spills are likely to occur over and over again, wall-to-wall carpeting is not practical. I have a painted floor cloth in my dining room . . . I'll explain later.

Window treatments

Again, as in the living room, make choices now about whether you'll use drapes or café curtains or blinds, etc. Will you have elaborate wrought-iron rods or simple wood ones? Your style—Elegant or Sporty—will dictate.

Lighting

The lighting in most dining rooms is usually a chandelier or some kind of overhead lighting. This is to properly light the center of the room, where the table is most likely situated, and to keep the fixture out of the way so people don't bump into it when walking around the table. There is probably some sort of ceiling fixture already in place in your dining room, so the decision may be as simple as keeping what's there or replacing it. You might also think about recessed lighting . . . or no lighting . . . I once used only candles in my dining room. It's not the norm, but that's the fun part of decorating.

Bedrooms

Paint: walls and trim, or wallpaper

If you plan to paint the walls, choose the color carefully but don't be afraid to change the color if in the end it doesn't work. And remember, in bedrooms, you have to choose the linens first. It's easier to find a paint color to match a comforter than the other way around. If you choose wallpaper for your bedroom, you have to be sure before you apply it—so see Chapter Seven for wallpaper ideas before you begin.

Bed

In choosing bed sizes, consider the people who will sleep in them and the dimensions of the room. Chances are you already have beds you can use, so you might use the style of the beds as a starting point for your design. You can change things around a little, though. You might build a platform for the bed, remove the head and footboards, and use big pillows instead. There's lots to think about.

Bed tables

You will need a table on at least one side of the master bed and maybe one on the side of a twin bed in your child's room. They can be tables made for that purpose or small dressers or small storage trunks. They don't have to match exactly the color or the style of the beds. Nor, if you have two tables, do they need to match each other. In my bedroom in New York I have a round table draped with fabric on one side and a small trunk on the other. Think beyond the expected.

Flooring

Make the decision between area rugs or wall-to-wall, and then choose the color by thinking about who is using the room. White carpeting in the master bedroom will look elegant, but put that white rug in the hallway and kids' rooms, and it will soon turn black. Save yourself the trouble of constant shampooing by choosing dark colors for high-traffic areas and rooms likely to get dirty.

Window treatments

The basics for a bedroom can include blinds to hide the early morning sun. You can use *only* blinds or can add curtains over them. Choose the color of the blinds carefully (it has to be one of your three basic colors) if they are going to be a backdrop for curtains with a pattern that has many colors. Think about wood blinds as an alternative.

Lighting

There may already be a ceiling light fixture in bedrooms, but you don't want that to be the only light in the room (you can use the same fixture to install a ceiling fan later, or you can remove the fixture). If you read in bed, some kind of bedside lamp is essential; for kids' rooms, a wall sconce placed high enough to be out of reach of little hands is a good solution (it provides softer light and won't get in the way of play).

Family Room

Paint: walls and trim, wallpaper or paneling

Many families like wood paneling for a room that gets so much high-energy use, and there are many types on the market that are a big step above that plastic-looking stuff from the seventies. If you already have wood paneling but don't like it, painting over it creates a country cottage look. There are also great washable wallpapers available.

Couches, chairs, sleepers

Since many family rooms double as guest rooms, consider buying a sleeper couch if you plan to have sleepovers. The furniture in this room should be comfy and durable. You will probably use many castoffs from other parts of the house here, so be careful to not let it look like a junkyard.

Entertainment center

It makes your room sound a little like Disney World, but an entertainment center is really just a place to put all of your electronic stuff. You may use an old armoire to house your TV, VCR, Nintendo games, and stereo, or you may have custom cabinets and shelves made. What you shouldn't do is have all that equipment strewn all over the room with various wires sprouting about for people to trip over.

You may also choose the family room to house your computer system. If you do, make sure it has a safe, attractive place to sit. Will you need a desk, file cabinets, shelves? Turning a closet into a little home office is a terrific idea because you can close the doors (and even lock them if you want) to hide your work space.

Toy storage

If your kids are of the age when they have toys everywhere, with what seems like millions of little pieces that seem to multiply themselves, you'll need some sort of storage plan for them. Children tend to take over every room, so if you have a well-thought-out storage plan for toys, you may be able to keep them contained. Sort through toys and see what you need by using ideas in Chapter Thirteen: Your Bedrooms.

Flooring

We're talking durable here. Whether it's an area rug over hardwood or tile floors, or wall-to-wall, this flooring will have to endure lots of traffic and spills.

Window treatments

You'll want something simple that the kids can operate and won't destroy. This doesn't mean that blinds and drapes can't be pretty; just put some thought into their function.

Lighting

For most activities, overhead lighting is the best solution in the family room; however, if the traffic will bear it, you can also have individual lamps. Another good option is track lighting or individual spots directed toward reading or work areas.

Bathrooms

Paint: walls and trim, or wallpaper

Bathrooms are one of my favorite rooms to work on because they are small and the work goes quickly. If you want to paint walls, make sure you choose a semi-gloss (flat latex paint will absorb water and streak), which dirt can be easily wiped from. For wallpaper, ask which styles are made specifically for bathrooms (some are too thin and will peel under steam). You need good ventilation in bathrooms (especially those with wallpaper) so if you don't have a fan, install one now.

Tile or prefabricated tub surround

You will need some sort of non-porous material on the walls to deflect water around the tub or shower. You can use a prefabricated tub surround (it's all one piece, including the walls, floor, and door) or tile on the walls. Chances are you will use what's already there, but if you are going to make a change, and want to choose a new tub surround, make sure it is in one of your three colors and matches your sink and toilet.

If you plan to start from scratch, this is where you can add colors and patterns. But don't forget to match the tiles to your fixture (tub, sink, etc., see below) color. Sometimes when all of the fixtures are white, we pretend they don't exist and forget that they are one of the three basic colors.

Bed & Bath Basics

I believe it's best to purchase things like towels, sheets, and other bed linens as you're assembling your basics. The reason is that you can always have paint mixed to match linens but may not be able to find the exact color linens to match paint (or wallpaper). I once envisioned a red, white, and blue bathroom. I finished all the decorating and then went out to find bright-red towels. I could never find the right shade of red. Some were too pink; some were too brown. The only true red towels I found were very thin and cheap-looking, and I wouldn't buy them. In the end, I settled for blue towels, but every time I went into that bathroom I kicked myself because I knew red was the color that would tie the whole room together. ❖

Toilet, sink, tub, faucets, vanity cabinet, medicine chest or mirror

A few rules: The toilet, sink, and tub must be the same color porcelain. White or off-white are less expensive than brighter colors, and they go well with everything; you're safer choosing white or off-white. Sink faucets should match shower/bath faucets in style (chrome sink faucet, chrome shower/bath faucet, etc.).

The vanity cabinet (the thing that holds the sink) and the medicine chest/mirror can be anything from antiques to ultramodern. You need them for the bathroom to function, but you can be more creative in their style.

Flooring

Bathroom floors should be tiled or wood. Period. People in warmer climates tend to carpet them if the rest of the house is done in wall-to-wall, but I just don't get it. The carpet gets soggy and moldy and smelly. Wood or tiles (even press and peel do-it-yourselfers) are the way to go, with a natural fiber area rug—maybe even an antique—over it. If you want, you can use those rubber-backed, washable bathroom carpets that you cut to size; but I don't recommend them—they still end up looking grungy fairly quickly.

Window treatments

You may want blinds and shades for privacy, with curtains over them for style. Choose the fabric first and then match the color to the blinds.

Lighting

Lighting in the bathroom should be near the mirror. It can be a single fixture, such as a bar with four light bulbs in it, over the mirror, or perhaps two separate wall sconces framing the mirror. If your bathroom has only an overhead fixture, consider having the wiring moved. If you can't do that, at least replace the fixture with a simple bowl-shaped cover in clouded glass to keep it from being too harsh.

Kitchen

Of course, the kitchen is my favorite room. Maybe I should make mine more unattractive, then I wouldn't be so tempted to eat so much! This room is not really one that can be totally accommodated by basics alone (although it still needs things like paint, wallpaper, and flooring). There are so many variables: cabinets, appliances, shelves, lighting, tile, etc. But have no fear; I have included an entire chapter just on kitchens to walk you through it. Turn to page 147 for guidance.

Basic Tools

Assemble a toolbox as soon as you move into your home. Having the right supplies on hand (and knowing where they are) will save time and money. If you don't know what some of these items are, take this list to a hardware store and ask for help. Don't be intimidated. (For you single ladies . . . it's a great place to meet men!)

- ❖ Slotted screwdriver
- ❖ Phillips head screwdriver
- ❖ Hammer
- ❖ Mallet (a wood or plastic hammer to tap things like molding into place without damaging wood)
- ❖ Handsaw
- ❖ Wrench
- ❖ Pliers
- ❖ File
- ❖ Scissors (good quality)
- ❖ Clamps (at least two, four if you can afford them)
- ❖ Tape measure, yardstick, and ruler
- ❖ Drill/Screw gun (cordless if you can)
- ❖ Sandpaper (in light and heavy grits)
- ❖ Electric sander (a pad sander or a rotary sander if you can afford it)
- ❖ Rubber gloves (buy a box of 100 at a surgical supply store)
- ❖ Masking tape
- ❖ Duct tape (you can fix anything with duct tape)
- ❖ Staple gun
- ❖ Hot-glue gun
- ❖ A box of Molly bolts (those things you stick in the wall to hold heavy items like shelves or towel bars)
- ❖ Paintbrushes (a variety of sizes)
- ❖ Paint roller (with stick extension for ceilings)
- ❖ Paint thinner
- ❖ Spray adhesive (comes in a can like spray paint)
- ❖ Plenty of rags (old T-shirts or diapers)

A Lot to Think About

I AM SURE that, after having read this chapter, your head is spinning and you're thinking, *Geez, this is a lot of work.* Decorating your home *is* a lot of work, but it doesn't all have to be done today or even tomorrow. What's important is that you have a plan and know what you're working toward. If you made your sample boards and have started a list of what you need to do or buy to accomplish your goals, you're halfway there. About that list: When you organized and cleaned your house (and I know you did this), you made a list of what you already have and where it will go. Now you know what you need to complete your basics. Compare the two lists and make a third list for each room that reflects everything you will need to buy. Carry this list with you everywhere (tape it to the back of your sample board for each room). Tuck all of your boards and lists in a notebook and let's go shopping. See you at the home center. . . .

Chapter 5

Secrets to Shop With

Y ou've made your sample boards and you've made your lists . . . now it's time to make your budget and plan when you will be able to afford each item on your list. If you're on a tight budget, creativity and careful shopping can make up for a lot. Your list is your friend, and you must take it with you everywhere. Here's why: Say you're shopping at Home Depot for kitchen cabinets, and you discover two bathroom sinks that are less than half price because someone else returned them and they are not in boxes. They're off-white and, how convenient, you need two off-white sinks for the master bathroom. What a great find. But there are lots of shades of off-white . . . will these match the off-white of your toilet and tub? If only you could remember the brand (colors within brands match) of your toilet and tub, then you'd know. You can't just buy these sinks and return them if they're not right, because they're a final sale. What to do? Well, I know what you *should* do. Look at your list and sample board. You've written down everything you need to know, including the name of the manufacturer of your bathroom fixtures. You're so smart! They're an exact match. Congratulations, you've just saved yourself over $200! Also, if you buy ones that are a different white, for the rest of your life in this house you'll walk into that bathroom and hate yourself that you bought two sinks that don't really match . . . and then who cares that you saved $200?

You'll see over and over again how this kind of organization will make shopping for home items easier. There are so many places to buy things both new and used that it does take some planning and restraint to make sure you get it right with the fewest number of mistakes. Your sample boards and lists will help. *I'll* help by telling you which things to buy first, where in your home to invest in quality, and how to do everything you want to do within your budget. This chapter is about shopping: where to go, how to buy, what to buy, etc. In later chapters, you'll find even more ideas about buying specific items like flooring, wallpaper, and window treatments. Whew . . . it's a lot to do. (And you thought dressing yourself was hard!)

Where to Start

AFTER YOU HAVE reorganized your home and decided what you want each room to look like, you have to put the basics in place. This means painting the walls, installing flooring, and acquiring the pieces of furniture that you will have for a long time. Accessories and accents come last, so don't even think about them now (although, if you see the exact mirror you want and it's on sale now, snap it up if you can, but don't go looking for extras just yet). Before you start to shop for your basic needs, read through this chapter to decide where you will shop for the most value. Then turn to the chapters devoted to specific items for tips on buying.

There are millions of places and ways to spend your money. Here's a rundown of what to expect from each:

Superstores

At some point, you'll have to decide between shopping the superstores or using your local businesses. It's a toss-up because the superstores like Home Depot and Ikea often offer the best prices, but local stores can take more time to answer your questions. And, if there is a problem (perhaps something you may even go to small-claims court over), stores in your community are more likely to settle quickly to preserve their reputation. I have found that the best way to decide between the two types of stores is to comparison shop. If you find two like items and your local store is the more expensive, at least offer them the option of meeting the lower price. Here's a sample dialogue for you to follow: *I would really like to support local businesses, but I can't afford to. I'd like to buy such-and-such, and I'd like to buy it from you. Can you meet their price? Do you provide free delivery?* (This can often make up the price difference right away.)

I have found that most businesses will jump at the chance to make a sale, and the fact that you gave them the opportunity to meet the superstore's price will be appreciated.

Now that's not to say that you shouldn't shop the superstores (are you confused yet?)—especially if the store is close by—only that I think you will get better service from a local business. For some items, it really pays to buy from the big guys. Some of the departments—kitchens, bathrooms—are set up to give you excellent service as well as lower prices. Basic supplies like paintbrushes and wallpaper paste will also be cheaper at the superstores because they buy in larger quantities. Also, take advantage of the many free clinics, demonstrations, and samples the superstores offer. You may learn enough to complete a project yourself and save on contractor fees.

Before making a trip to a superstore, go over your lists again and make a separate list of what you hope to get there. If you can afford to get everything on your new list at once, do it, you'll save on delivery charges. Try not to fall into the trap of wandering around the store, tossing things into your cart that aren't on your list—these stores make a lot of money off of your impulse buys and display items in a way to feed into them. Those ten shrubs that you decide you must have this minute are going to throw your budget out of whack. We're not working on the landscaping today, so don't buy the shrubs. Don't even think about it.

If you would like to speak with a consultant or in-house decorator (these services are usually free, and you should take advantage of them), call ahead to make an appointment. Avoid weekends to beat the crowds. Don't be shy about asking the consultant to show you all the options, even if it takes all day. You won't be ready to buy until you've seen and priced everything. Actually, I strongly recommend that you take samples (or at least pictures) home and look at them in the rooms they are intended for before you sign any con-

Buying on Sale

Frank and I helped my son and daughter-in-law decorate their home. The master bedroom is all off-whites and creams. Laura found a pile of pillow shams on sale for $5 each and bought a bunch. Trouble was, none were the right shade of off-white. Some were mustardy, some were pinkish, some greenish. Sure she saved a bundle (the shams were originally $30 each), but so what? She couldn't use the shams, and they were a final sale. If she had brought a sample of the fabric with her, she never would have made this mistake and wasted all that time and money. Don't buy just because something is on sale. It's really just like clothes—it's not a good deal unless it really works. ❖

tracts to buy. Here's the phrase of the week: "Let me think about it." In fact, this should be part of your everyday lexicon. If you are planning to use a contractor to install items such as kitchen cabinets, show the samples to him and by all means, make him do the measuring so he'll be responsible (put it in writing) if something doesn't fit.

Regular Stores (including chains)

The advantages of small stores (as opposed to superstores) is that they usually have one-of-a-kind merchandise and will offer superior service. Each sale is very important to them. Some stores, like Ethan Allen, even have in-house decorators who will work with you without charge. They will help you match wallpaper and paint and carpeting to the furniture they sell. Stores like Sears or JCPenney tend to make items in matching colors in all of their departments. They will have carpet that matches their sofas and towels that go with bathroom rugs. You're more on your own at a store like this, but at least they try to make it easy for you.

Employees of your local hardware stores can be your best friends. Try to establish a relationship with them. Tell them what your project is and let them know you'll be stopping in for supplies a lot. These people know how to use all of the items they sell and are happy to offer advice on everything from installing window shades to selecting crown molding. My local hardware store is owned and run by two sisters. I feel so comfortable there because they never treat me like an idiot. (Male employees at other stores tend to give me the "Okay, honey . . ." routine. Don't let them do it to you. Tuck this book under your arm and march right in, because now you know what you're doing.) I shop there often just to support them, even though they're a little more expensive than other places. However, they repay my loyalty by patiently answering all of my stupid questions. That counts for a lot.

Also, many small hardware stores have banded together to buy merchandise jointly so they can offer lower prices and compete with the superstores. Stores that include True Value and ServiStar in their names are part of just such a co-op.

Catalogs

I can't believe the number of catalogs there are now for home items. Their growth over the last few years has been amazing. You have to be careful when ordering from catalogs because the returns are so bulky; however, if you order correctly, there are some great deals and unique items. If you haven't heard of them yet, here are a few to try. Call the toll-free number listed to receive a copy of their catalog. Some charge a small fee for the catalog that can be applied to an order.

Ballard Designs   (800-367-2775)

Furniture, lamps, rugs, fabric, frames, mirrors, and other unique accessories.

Calico Corners   (800-213-6366)

Fabrics, curtain rods, ready-made pillows.

Chambers   (800-334-9790)

Highest-quality linens and towels, unique lamps, and other bedroom accessories.

Crate & Barrel   (800-323-5461)

Furniture, lighting, glassware also available in their retail stores. Some items catalog exclusive.

Domestications   (800-746-2555)

Linens, curtains, lamps, rugs, other accessories for the bed and bath.

Exposures   (800-222-4947)

Unique picture frames and mirrors. Photo-storage accessories and wood shelving.

Frontgate   (800-626-6488)

Outdoor furniture and accessories, unique wood storage units and desks, kitchen and bath accessories.

Hold Everything   (800-421-2264)

Storage solutions for everything; many are beautiful pieces.

Home Decorators Collection (800-245-2217)

Lamps, tables, rugs, many one-of-a-kind items.

Orac Decor   (800-526-0462)

Polyurethane cornice, panel and chair rail moldings, ceiling medallions, columns, pilasters, wall light fixtures, decorations, pediments, door and wall surrounds, pedestals and corbels.

Pottery Barn   (800- 922-5507)

Furniture, lamps, rugs and other items available in their retail stores and other catalog-exclusive items.

Ross-Simons Gift & Home Collection   (800-458-4545)

Furniture, small hand-painted chests, dinnerware, linens, rugs, outdoor furniture.

Ru de France   (800-777-0998)

French Country furniture, decorative hardware, linens, accessories.

Smith & Noble Window Ware   (800-248-8888)

Curtains, fabric, blinds and shades.

The Company Store   (800-285-3696)

Linens, luscious comforters, towels. Variety of colors is exceptional.

This End Up   (800-627-5161)

Furniture available in their retail stores and other items only sold through the catalog.

Williams-Sonoma   (800-541-2233)

Everything for your kitchen and dining room, including small appliances, dinnerware, tablecloths, etc.

Antique Stores

If you love old things as I do, you'll be spending a lot of time in antique stores, browsing and getting to know the owners. Of course, the further away from big cities you can go, the better the prices will be. If you have some idea of what you want—the period, the style—it pays to buy and study a pricing guide so you aren't going in blind. There are many on the market, from ones that cover a broad spectrum of antiques to those that are specific to one style. Check them out of your local library and then photocopy the pages you are interested in.

Another group of handy publications are those that list antique stores and auction houses. These books are usually written to appeal to specific regions of the country, such as the Northwest or Midwest, etc. They, too, are available at most libraries.

You really have to know the market before you plunk down some cash for what you think are antiques. I hate to say this, but you can't count on antiques sellers to be scrupulously honest about the provenance and condition of the piece (although most are), especially if it's a private owner (they may not really know and are just repeating what someone told them). Most antiques are sold "as is," so be sure to examine whatever you buy carefully. I suggest starting small, buying a few inexpensive accessories or small tables, before moving on to major pieces. I never buy an antique without asking a dealer or another crazy collector for advice.

Flea Markets/Tag Sales

There's nothing more exciting than a huge field filled with tables of things for sale. It's almost like finding a warehouse of Donna Karans at half price. Although you can make spectacular finds at flea markets and tag sales, you can also make mistakes by impulse buying and turning yourself right into a Junk Collector. You do know that one person's junk is another's treasure, right? Good. Just make sure you don't take one person's junk and make it your junk.

The good news is that you can save a ton of money by picking up others' castoffs if you shop wisely. You have to bring your sample boards and lists with you even if you are going to a garage sale. Even if it's cheap, cheap, cheap, you're still not allowed to buy anything that is not on your list.

Remember that flea markets and tag sales are almost always three things: cash, carry, and final sale. So make sure you bring cash (a good way to stick to your budget is to bring only as much as you can afford to spend), have some way to carry your purchases home, and last, spend some time thinking about your purchase before you hand over your money. Once you've made the big decision, do try to negotiate the price a bit. It's expected and the person doing the selling has most likely priced the item a little above his final price. If you're at a moving sale, negotiate a little harder. The seller wants to get rid of his stuff and may be a little more flexible.

One last reminder: Be sure that you are buying what you need, and that you won't be selling that same item at *your* garage sale next year.

Cheap Thrills

When Liberace was alive, he was a flea-market hound. It gave him such pleasure to pick up a fifty-cent tchotchke and then have it plated in either silver or brass and place it next to something from Tiffany's. His cheap thrills were just as valuable to him as a Ming vase. He got the biggest charge when someone would ask him where he bought his treasures. He never gave away his secret, but smiled to himself over his little trick for making something out of nothing. ❖

Auctions

You can pick up great things at great prices at auctions. You've probably heard or read about big celebrity auctions like the one for Jackie Onassis's belongings and are right now thinking, *Is Linda crazy? I could never afford to shop at an auction.* But listen, just because that type of auction is not for you doesn't mean that there aren't some that are. Most of the auctions in this country are run by small auction houses or are private sales of the belongings in one house. These auctions are terrific. You can find out about them by checking listings in your local papers, or by looking in the library for directories of auction houses. A simple phone call to them will give you the dates and contents of particular auctions.

The best part of these smaller auctions is that the people bidding are probably just like you, on a limited budget but with good taste. So it may take some patience before you find things you want for your home that other people don't outbid you for (let them—you have a budget), but you will eventually get them if you persist.

There are a few rules about auctions that you should know before you go:

❖ Read the rules posted on the door or registration desk before you go in. This auction may be cash only. No credit cards or checks.

❖ You often have to register before you are given a number. Your number may be on a wooden paddle or simply written on a piece of paper. When you bid, you raise your number so the auctioneer can record your bid.

❖ Ask if there is a buyer's premium. That means that the auction house will collect between five and twenty percent of the purchase price as their profit. If so, figure it into your budget because it can add up. If you buy $500 worth of merchandise, you could owe an additional $100 if the premium is twenty percent.

❖ Always attend the preview of the auction merchandise before the bidding begins. Purchases are final and the condition is "as is," so you must really inspect things before you bid.

❖ Establish your top bid before you raise your number. You have to know when you'll stop bidding and bow out. It's easy to get caught up in the frenzy of the auction, so if you find it difficult to back down, you might bring a friend to restrain your competitive urges.

Just Say No

———

When Frank and I were decorating our previous apartment in New York, we were really pressed for time and decided to hire a decorator to find a few specific pieces for the living room. The decorator had all the right credentials and came very highly recommended, so when he appeared at our door with two burgundy chairs we let him in and paid him. I hated the chairs, Frank hated the chairs, but we were both afraid to say anything because this decorator had done all the research and knew what he was doing. Was it our taste that was bad? We ended up living with those chairs for ten years before we finally had to admit that we made a mistake and should have sent them back immediately. Just because the decorator says it's so, doesn't mean it is. If you don't like something, say so. ❖

❖ You will be responsible for carting your prize home unless the auction house offers delivery (for a price, of course), so be prepared with a van or truck.

Sometimes You Need a Hand

THERE ARE DEFINITELY times when it's wiser to ask for help when designing or renovating a room. If you have a particular style in mind, you may want to hire a decorator to help you find all of the pieces if you don't have the time to track them down yourself. You may also want a decorator if you are truly stumped and need a little help jump-starting your imagination.

There are many jobs I think you can do yourself—painting, tiling, installing wood flooring, putting up wainscotting or a chair rail—but there are others—putting in new windows or skylights, cutting and installing a granite countertop, making built-in bookcases—for which hiring a contractor is a better way to go.

Here's an overview of what decorators and contractors can do for you, and tips on how to hire them and monitor their work.

Decorators

Do you need a decorator? Will it save you money in the long run? It's hard to say without knowing you, but I certainly can say that if you are on a very limited budget, you should work as your own decorator and invest your time instead of your money. Careful shopping and your creativity can achieve a lot.

However, should you go this route, here's what decorators do and how they charge for their services. Ideally a decorator will spend a lot of time with you and go over each detail. You can have them work only on the basics and simple plans or provide everything down to the books on your shelves. I believe that the search for all of the extras that personalize a room is part of the fun, and I would never let anyone else do it for me, but if you're strapped for time or can't ever trust your own instincts, a decorator can help. You shouldn't feel bad if you just don't have the "eye" for decorating. You're smart enough to know that you need help.

Decorators can charge for their services in four ways: 1) They will take a percentage of the total cost of the job, usually twenty-five percent. Typically, you will pay only wholesale prices for furniture if you do it this way. This type of fee arrangement works best if you have a huge project that includes three or four rooms, top to bottom; 2) They charge you retail for the items they buy and keep anything above their wholesale cost as their fee. If you are looking for a few really nice pieces of furniture, this can pay off because you are paying what you would for the piece anyway and you get the decorator's advice for free; 3) By the hour. If you just need help getting the basics in place and have a pretty clear idea of what you want, this can pay off by having the decorator do the legwork and buying after you make the choices; and 4) A flat fee. This type of fee arrangement can work out the best if you are on a limited budget. You'll know exactly what the final cost will be before you start.

As with any other contractor, you need to put everything in writing. Not because you don't trust them, but so the decorator will know what your expectations are and you will know exactly what services the decorator will provide. Write *everything* down. The relationship may start out friendly, but differences of opinion do happen and tempers may even become frayed. If so, you can point to your contract and insist you get what you paid for.

Put It in Writing

I know I have told you a million times to put everything in writing when dealing with a contractor, but here's one of the many reasons why. A friend was doing a renovation and had decided on a contractor. When they were walking around the house, she mentioned other small jobs that needed to be done. The contractor said, *Yeah, I'll throw that in, I'll throw that in,* etc. When she got the contract, none of these items were listed but she figured that was okay because the contractor said he'd do them. As the job went on, things got tense because it was way behind schedule. There were a few arguments, things had to be redone, etc. When my friend mentioned the extras, the contractor said he was willing to do only what was in the contract. Well, my friend hadn't really negotiated down the price because she felt the extras were worth it, but now she wouldn't be getting anything extra. The whole relationship fell apart at this point, and she couldn't wait to get the contractor out of her house. She felt really taken, but learned next time to write down *everything* no matter how trivial it may seem. ❖

Contractors

Speaking of contractors (and by this I mean *any* person who is performing labor in your home), this is an item that you also have to shop for in the same careful way as you might for the perfect dining room table. After all, this is a person that is going to be working in your home and fulfilling your vision. Use the following guidelines to select a contractor:

1) Ask friends for references. If you see an addition or a kitchen that is well done, ask who did the work.

2) Ask other contractors for references. Contractors often subcontract jobs out or work with other companies. So if someone has hung wallpaper in your bathroom for you and you ask them if they know a good plumber, they'll usually suggest someone trustworthy.

3) Hire only licensed contractors. Each municipality has different rules for issuing licenses to work in their area. Call your town's building inspector to check out the contractor's history. If there is a problem later on, the office that issued the license will often help you seek restitution (at the very least, they'll know where the contractor lives).

4) Insist upon insurance. Large companies will have an umbrella policy that covers their employees and any damage that might occur in your home. Smaller companies can take out a policy specific to each job. Make sure you get a copy of the policy before work starts. If someone is injured in your home, you could be liable if they don't have insurance.

5) Try to hire locally. People who live and work in your town will have more of a reason to live up to their word. They are less willing to put their reputation at stake in their own backyard. Also, if you end up with a dispute, you can use your local small-claims court to resolve the problem. You must file such suits where the contractor lives, not where you live. If that's a hundred miles away, it can be very inconvenient. Of course, this will never happen to you after you read this book . . . but just in case.

6) Interview at least three contractors for the job, ask them for references, and then call those references. Usually people like to help, so don't be embarrassed to pick up the phone. Ask contractors to put their bids in writing and then compare like costs. Compatibility counts for a lot here, after all, this person is going to be in your house, but price also counts. If you want to work with a certain person, but their price is too high, maybe you can use the other bids to negotiate. Don't be shy . . . take a deep breath . . . and ask if specific costs can be brought down. Very often the contractor will agree.

7) Once you have decided on a contractor, get *everything* in writing. I mean *everything*. No matter how nice someone may seem, when it comes down to dollars and cents, you both have to be clear about what is expected. The contract should include:

❖ The cost of the work and what the finished result should be. I suggest doing this item by item, separating materials and labor. The contractor should charge you whatever he paid for materials without a markup; his fee should come from the labor.

❖ The timeline and fee schedule for the job. A down payment of no more than a third of the total should be due at signing, and then create benchmarks for the contractor to meet before receiving further payment, reserving at least a quarter of the total for when the job is completely done. If it is a large job, you might even put in a penalty clause if the contractor is not done by a certain date, say $100 per day he goes over.

❖ Any specifics that are important to you. I prefer to have the contractor cart away any refuse even if that means I have to pay a little more. Most contractor waste (wood, Sheetrock, etc.) is not accepted in regular garbage pickup, and I'd rather not have to make a trip to the dump myself. I also like the job site to be cleaned every night so I'm not stepping on nails or tripping over pipes (Frank actually does this himself because he's so immaculate). Write down what you expect. I also don't like it if a contractor works two days at my house, then goes off for two days at another house, and then comes back to finish my job. I like them to work straight through. State in the contract that they will work every day from eight to four until the job is completed.

❖ Write down who will be performing the work. You may have interviewed the owner of the company and liked him, but someone different will be doing the actual work. Ask who they are and how long they have been working for the contractor. When you call references ask exactly who performed the work (describe him; the name Bob may not be enough).

Chapter 6

The Magic of Paint

Paint is everything. It is the most important basic element of a room and it is also the most fun to play with (not to mention the least expensive part of decorating your home). The beauty of paint is two-part: Anyone can apply it (even you), and anyone can re-apply it if the finished effect isn't right. And re-apply it and re-apply it. Of course, we'll work toward you getting it right the first time, but if you don't, it really doesn't matter because it's so simple to change, add to, or totally re-do. It's kind of like changing your lipstick. You put on a shade of pink and then look in the mirror. Oops! You're wearing an orange shirt . . . pink won't do . . . wipe it off and start over. Paint is the same way.

What can you paint? EVERYTHING. Walls, trim, moldings, doors, floors, furniture, mirror frames, drawer pulls, even tile . . . the list is endless. You can take it as far as your imagination can go. You can use paint purely as a background for your rooms or you can make it an integral element of your design. You can use many colors or just one. You can do special effects, draw murals, stencil borders . . . again, you can paint anything your mind can think of and that you have the stamina for. Don't shy away! Even the most physically inept person can paint a room themselves (and it's worth it to do basic painting yourself, with professional painters costing $200 and up per room) and learn the techniques that make paint special.

When my first husband and I were married, we bought a little house in Long Beach, California, a tiny cottage really. We scraped together enough for a down payment, but then there wasn't a cent left over for decorating. We gathered used furniture where we could, and I bought inexpensive fabric to brighten it up, but it was paint that truly transformed this so-so place into a "Wow! How did you do that?" home. At the time it was standard to use a pale color on walls and always, always, white paint on the window trim and baseboards. Every single house I ever saw was the same. I decided to try something different. I painted all of the wood trim in colors. Blues, greens, yellows. I chose my accent color (one of my basic colors) in each room and used that color on the trim. The color matched the stripes on the throw pillows or the flowers in the curtains or the knobs on the kitchen cabinets. I said goodbye to white and hello to a whole new idea in decorating. My rooms looked finished. They didn't have that glare of standard white that stood out like a beacon. The colors were brighter, but because they fit into the overall scheme of the room, you barely noticed them. You only noticed that they worked. And you know what? Even if other people didn't like the look (but they did), I loved it, and that's all that mattered.

I know that some of you will have a hard time getting away from white. White walls, white trim. You may even live in a rental that prohibits you from painting any color other than white. You can handle it two ways: You can ask your landlord for permission to change colors, with a promise to repaint them white before you move, or you can use white as one of your three basic colors. Most people who paint walls white then block it out. They think of white as a neutral noncolor that doesn't count. It does. You have to somehow tie it in to your furniture and accessories. Don't think, *I painted everything white, now I need lots of bright colors to offset it.* If you have a bright blue-and-green couch, tie it into the white walls by making white pillows trimmed in blue or green. You'll see, all of a sudden, this small change will make the room work together.

When it comes to color, you have to go with what you like and what will make you happy over time. I have a friend whose very large master bedroom is painted orange. Not a bright, gaudy orange, but a vibrant darkish shade of salmony orange. When her husband first saw

Too Much Color

Another celebrity . . . I can't tell you her name . . . because, well, you'll see . . . painted her living room white and then felt that she had to bring in every other color under the sun to counter the blank walls. The room looks like a pair of golf pants. Truly, it's a disaster. She overdid the other colors instead of thinking about a plan that included painting the walls. I think she was afraid to go anywhere other than white and, as a result, went everywhere. Don't use white as a safety net . . . it rarely works. ❖

the paint chip he was extremely dubious. He decided to let her try it and see how it looked, but he was really thinking, *Forget it.* She painted the walls and the cathedral ceiling all the same color, then moved in the furniture and accessories. The next morning her husband woke up in the room and thought, *Hey, she was right, this is fantastic.* The morning sun streaming in the windows made the room feel rosy and bright—it made him feel that way, too. They still get plenty of comments from visitors like, "*This* is an *interesting* color," but they don't care because they love it. That's really what it's all about. Do you love it?

Buying Paint

PAINT CAN COST ANYWHERE from $7.99 a gallon to $25.99 a gallon or even more for designer brands. Is there a difference? Actually there is: Generally the more expensive paint will be thicker. Does that mean you should buy the more expensive one? Not necessarily. If you're painting a flat wall and using a less expensive paint, you'll probably have to use more coats to get the coverage you want. However, if you're painting a textured wall, piece of furniture, etc., you'll want the thinner paint so that the texture shows through. Shop smart, keeping in mind the job at hand.

Buy all the paint you need for a room at the same time, particularly if you are having a color mixed. Write down the color code and paint brand on your sample board right away. Even if you are buying white, there are many different kinds of white and it won't be easy to match unless it is exactly the same.

Buy only as much paint as you need. Having extra gallons in the basement won't help anyone. If you are doing a decorative effect such as washing you'll need only a quart, not a gallon, so plan ahead.

Paint goes on sale pretty regularly, especially at the superstores, so it pays to wait for a sale and then buy for the whole house at once. Do this with supplies also. Buy all roller covers and brushes at once if they are on sale.

For regular painting of the walls and trim I suggest you use disposable foam brushes for the corners where the roller won't reach. They're cheap (they range from 35 to 85 cents apiece) and easy to use. They don't leave bristle marks and the pointed edge is great for neatly painting the line between the wall and the ceiling. Best of all you don't have to clean them.

My last piece of advice is this: Don't choose paint when you're feeling gray. It's like shopping when you feel hungry. You load up your cart with food, any kind of food, every kind of food. When you get home, you see that you have nothing good to eat, so you just eat junk and more junk. If you pick out paint when you're not feeling inspired, the same thing will happen. You won't focus on what you really want, and you'll pick some color that will never work in your home just to get it over with. Shop for paint when you're in a good mood.

Glossy or Matte, Latex or Oil?

Paint comes in an infinite variety of textures and mixtures, and choosing the right one for the job is important. Here's a list of the paints found in most stores:

Exterior: Paints designed to withstand weather. To be used on the exterior of your home.

Glaze: A transparent oil- or water-based paint that allows the base-coat color to show through. Used for the top coat in ragging, marbling, combing.

Glaze tint: The solid color pigments to be mixed with glaze.

Glossy: Has a high shine. Can be more difficult to apply than semi-gloss because texture is thicker and may leave roller marks on wall. Easy to clean stains and spots when dry. Use this or semi-gloss in the kitchen, bathroom, family room, kids' rooms, anywhere you need an easy-to-clean surface. Can use in other rooms where you want a super high-gloss finish as a design element.

Interior: Paints designed to be used inside your home.

Latex: Water-based paint. Comes in flat, semi-gloss, or glossy. Easy to apply and clean up while using.

Oil-based: Color pigments are mixed with oil. Requires paint thinner or turpentine to remove from hands and brushes. Rarely used any more because water-based paints have improved durability. When using an oil-based glaze, directions often call for an oil-based coat, but I haven't found this to make a difference.

Primer: A sealant that is applied under base coat. Used to protect surface from humidity and dirt and to better cover old paint before new color is applied. You would use over brand-new Sheetrock or plaster to seal before you paint.

Semi-gloss: Has some shine to it—midway between flat and glossy—and is easy to apply and wipe clean of spots when dry. Use in kitchen, bathrooms, kids' rooms, family room, anywhere you want an easy-to-clean surface.

Water-based: Color pigments are mixed with water. Dries faster than oil-based and is easier to clean off hands and brushes.

Walls and Trim

BY NOW YOU'VE collected color chips and magazine pages and probably have a good idea of how you want each room to look. You know what your basic colors are and what your accent colors are. It's time to get rolling, literally.

I think paint can affect you emotionally when you walk into a room. It's the essence of the space. It can create illusions. You really want to get this right, so here are a few things to think about. Remember that paint goes on darker than it looks in the can. The best way to find out how your room will look is to paint the inside of a closet. Really. All my closets have been painted at least twice. Clear out the clothes and paint all four walls in the color you want to try. If you hate it in the closet, you'll hate it in your bedroom. Paint the closet again. When you love it, start on your chosen room.

Applying Paint to Walls

Painting a room yourself is really fairly straightforward. I know you can do it. The key to a neat, professional-looking job lies in the preparation of the room and walls and in planning your painting strategy. To prepare, remove as much furniture as you can from the room and cover the rest with tarps or old blankets.

Wash the ceilings and walls with soap and water and let dry. Scrape away any old, loose paint from walls and trim. Use spackling paste to fill in uneven areas left over after scraping. Let paste dry and sand to a smooth finish.

If you are painting the ceiling, do it first. Mask off any molding near ceiling that you intend to paint in a different color. Start in one corner, use a brush to paint at wall edge (about four inches in), and then roll in straight lines, covering area you painted with brush to blend. Use gentle pressure on the roller so that you don't create lines in between each roll. If you see lines, smooth them out as you go. Once dry, the lines will be visible.

The Right Tape

Don't ever use masking tape to make a straight edge between the wall and the ceiling or the wall and the window molding. It's much too sticky. I know. I've spent hours peeling itsy-bitsy pieces off. Instead, use the less sticky tape available in hardware stores that's made just for this job. It's easy to use and comes in very wide widths for messy painters. ❖

If you paint the walls next, you will not need to mask off all window casings and baseboards. Don't worry about getting paint on them now because you will go over them later. For walls, use the same technique of brushing paint in corners, before rolling. At the ceiling, use a straightedge (they are made just for this job and you can buy them in hardware stores for about $1 each) to apply paint and create a sharp line between wall and ceiling. Roll over the area you brushed (as close as you can get without touching ceiling) to blend edges. Always roll vertically, apply gentle pressure, and do areas about four feet wide at a time. Step back and look at your work from time to time to check for drips and paint lines. Roll these out as you see them.

The very best way to paint trim is to remove it and paint it layed out on the floor and then rehang it. If you can't do this, wait until walls and ceiling are completely dry before beginning. Mask off all the walls around trim (using special tape available at hardware stores). On wide trim you can use a small roller (it applies more paint and leaves a smoother finish than brushes). For small areas of trim, use foam brushes because they won't leave bristle marks. If you get paint on window glass, let it dry and then scrape off with a utility knife (in your toolkit, right?). Painting trim takes patience. Lots of it. Give yourself the time to do a good job, because it will be noticed if it's messy.

Instant Chic

I once walked into a dining room that was stunning and the very best part about it was that it cost about $10 to transform nothing furniture into a showplace. The woman had an old wicker table which she spray-painted royal blue. She then bought four white director's chairs and sponge-painted them with royal-blue paint. Then, and this was the unifying detail, she bought simple white plates and sponge-painted them, also in royal blue, and hung them on the walls. The result was something you might see in a high-end decorating magazine. I still can't get over it. So simple, so elegant. ❖

Furniture

USING PAINT TO BRING new life to tired furniture is the easiest thing in the world. It's also an inexpensive way to add style to a room. What can you paint? Anything and everything. Chairs, tables, kitchen cabinets, lamps, frames . . . if you have it, you can paint it. Use some of the decorative painting techniques discussed later in this chapter for your own unique style (be sure to ask for glazes that work on wood).

If you have six dining-room chairs that don't match and you can't afford to buy six that do, painting them is a way to bring them all together. The individual styles of the chairs won't look so out-of-place if they are all the same color. Use a semi-gloss or glossy paint (cover with a coat of varnish for a super shiny look) so it won't rub off on unsuspecting diners.

Paint a piece of furniture in a way you'd never dream of doing. Take a small end table or a chair and experiment. You may see a picture of a chair in a bright kelly green with a cute blue-and-green-checked seat cover. You think, *I could never have that.* But you can. Try it. What's the harm? You can always repaint it. Try white with black trim next time. That's the beauty of paint. If you want to change your color scheme without spending a fortune, use paint.

If you want to try an antique look, apply decals (available at craft stores) before you paint. The best way to achieve a crackling, aged look is simple: Paint furniture with an oil-based paint and then, before it dries, cover with the same color water-based paint. As the oil dries underneath it will begin to crack. When both coats are dry, coat one more time with the oil-based paint. Instant antique.

Decorative Painting Techniques

GIVING TEXTURE TO YOUR walls and trim by using paint is an easy, inexpensive way to decorate. I've read many books on decorative painting and have tried to follow the instructions given. Boy, was that defeating. Unless you are a professional artist or are willing to pay a fortune to a professional, there is no way you could achieve the desired look based on those instructions. What I've done here is pare down the steps and the number of supplies you need. These are the tricks I've learned, but don't feel you have to follow even my instructions to the tee. If something works better for you, then that's what you should do. Try to remain flexible; you may love the result!

Rag Rolling

Other books will tell you to take an itsy-bitsy piece of cloth, twist it, and roll glaze over your base coat to create the desired effect (see photo). If you have weeks (I'm not kidding) to spare, be my guest. If you want the exact same look and have only an afternoon to complete the project, here's what to do:

Supplies Needed

Base-coat paint

Roller

Roller covers, 2 (one for base coat, one for glaze)

Roller trays, 2 (one for base coat, one for glaze)

Brushes

Rubber gloves

Drop cloth

Mixing medium

Glaze tint

Large, clean rag

Rubber bands

Large piece of scrap cardboard or poster board

Instructions

❖ Paint walls (or trim or whatever you intend to "rag") in base coat. You can use water- or oil-based flat paint. Allow to dry overnight. If previous color shows through, apply a second coat of base coat. Otherwise, one coat is fine.

❖ Mix glaze according to instructions. Mix a small amount at a time to keep it fresh while applying.

❖ Put a clean roller cover on roller. Take a large rag (an old cloth diaper is perfect) and twist it tightly. Wrap the rag around roller and secure with rubber bands (don't worry about indents left by rubber bands, they'll add to the texture left on walls).

❖ Roll in glaze and then roll on cardboard, once all the way around the roller, to remove excess glaze.

❖ Roll glaze onto wall randomly, changing direction with each roll. Keep rolling until all glaze is gone from rag. (Ragging looks best when some areas are heavy and some light, so don't worry if some spots have very little glaze on them. Also, you can go back after it dries and fill in spots with a small rag.)

❖ To do edges, use a small, twisted rag and roll by hand.

❖ Even though it's called "rag rolling," you don't necessarily have to use a rag. Try wrapping other things around a roller and test on a piece of cardboard. Some ideas to try: bubble wrap, a textured dish towel, paper.

Splattering

This effect is great for a kid's room or a bathroom. You're supposed to take a paintbrush and hit it with one hand, splattering paint on the walls. If you do it this way, you'll cover about a square yard an hour (and that's just one color!). Forget it; follow my advice instead. Here's how:

Supplies Needed:

Semi-gloss base-coat paint

Semi-gloss splatter coat (in your three colors)

Rubber gloves

Drop cloth

An empty spray bottle (an old Windex bottle works great)

Instructions

❖ Paint walls in base coat and let dry overnight.

❖ Cover window, trim, floors, and everything else you don't want splattered.

❖ Fill spray bottle about halfway with paint. Add about two tablespoons of water and shake bottle to mix (paint alone will be too thick to spray). Test spray on piece of cardboard or in a closet (make sure all the clothes are removed; you don't want to walk around looking like your walls). The further you stand from the wall, the smaller and more spread out the splatters will be; stand closer for larger and more concentrated splatters. Keep adding small amounts of water until you get the look you want, but be careful, too much water and you will get lots of drips.

❖ Clean and fill bottle with a second paint color if you choose (you can do as many as you like). Add water and splatter over first color. Don't get carried away. Because if you hate it . . . oh yeah . . . back to the first step . . . so know when to fold 'em.

Marbling

This is an effect best used in small spaces such as window moldings, fireplace mantels, or picture frames. It would take forever to faux-marble an entire wall, but it can be—and has been—done. This is probably one of the hardest decorative painting techniques, so if you don't have a lot of patience—and time— you should probably choose a different technique. I marbled a small vanity cabinet in my New York bathroom. It looks gorgeous, but it took forever to do.

Supplies (for green marble)

Semi-gloss latex paint for base coat—black, dark green, and white

Large sponges, 3 (carwash sponges work great)

Roller trays to hold paint, 4(three for semi-gloss, one for glaze)

Rubber gloves

Drop cloth

Clear glaze

Glaze tint—black, white, and green

One-inch-wide brush

Paint thinner

Half-inch-wide brush

Clean cotton rags

Feathers

Instructions

❖ Pour base-coat paints into three separate roller trays.

❖ Dip sponge in black paint and wring out. Apply paint as if you were washing surface (wide sweeps across, up and down, in circles, whatever pattern you like). Don't cover every single inch in black, you need to leave some space for the green.

❖ Before black paint completely dries, dip clean sponge into dark green paint and wring out excess. Wash green over the entire surface, over black and filling in holes.

Rag rolling is an easy painting technique that adds so much style to a room. (Wm. Zinsser & Co., Inc. Blend & Glaze faux finishing liquid. For free literature call (732) 469-4367.)

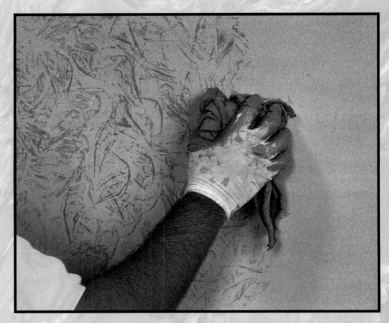

Splattering this hardwood floor and painting on some geometric shapes instantly adds interest to the room and makes it look oh-so-Modern. Isn't it a fun look?

Combing

adds texture and interest to your walls. You can drag the comb vertically, in a crisscross or wavy pattern (see inset)— really, in any pattern you like. Have fun with it!

(Martin Senour Paints 1-800-MSP-5270)

You can create

the look of marble anywhere in your home. Doesn't this room have a rich, Classic feel? Who would guess it's not real marble?

Sponging is simple but does take a long time. I think the effect is worth it, and what's a weekend of work when you'll have a room you'll enjoy for years? (Wm. Zinsser & Co., Inc. Blend & Glaze faux finishing liquid. For free literature call (732) 469-4367.)

In this room, the walls are washed in a cross-hatch pattern. Now isn't that better than plain white? (Martin Senour Paints 1-800-MSP-5270)

You can add stenciling

anywhere you want, and there are so many designs to choose from. If you can't find a stencil you like, make your own. Come on, be creative! This is your home; make it sing with your personality.

(MARTIN SENOUR PAINTS 1-800-MSP-5270)

❖ Make a lighter green by adding some green to the white until you come up with a color you like. Add about a half cup of water and mix thoroughly. Dip in sponge and really wring it out. Blot sponge on surface; don't wipe. This is where your opinion comes in. Sponge on as much light green as you want. Marble comes in all shades and variations, so experiment. (Of course, at this point it looks like a big mess and you're saying, *What have I done!* Don't worry, it'll look fine by the time you're finished.)

❖ Allow base coats to dry. Mix white and green glaze tint and add to clear glaze. Mix well. Dip in one-inch-wide brush and begin painting on wide vein patterns (you may want to use a real piece of marble for an idea of how this looks). After you've made all the veins, take the half-inch-wide brush and dip in paint thinner. Splatter over veins (not too much—you don't want drips) to spread glaze. Use clean rags to blot excess.

❖ Mix black tint with clear glaze. Dip in edges of a feather and then lightly wipe off excess on a clean cloth. Apply tiny veins by dragging feather along surface. Again, be creative. You can wiggle the feather a little, making long veins, short ones, ones with many offshoots. It's up to you.

❖ For a high-shine look, you can now varnish over entire surface a few times, allowing to fully dry between coats.

Combing

Combing, or dragging, objects through paint can leave an elegant, yet subtle design (depending on the colors you choose; obviously, a yellow base coat with a red glaze will be pretty bright). You can do an entire room, just one wall, or the wall above a chair rail. Use two closely matched shades for a soft, textured finish or a light and a dark shade for bold stripes. You can also create a parquet look by alternately combing small sections vertically than horizontally. You can also do zigzags (combing this way looks great on furniture). Because glaze must be wet when worked, it is easier to do this project with two people.

Supplies

Base-coat color

Roller

Roller covers, 2

Roller tray (wash in between uses)

Rubber gloves

Drop cloth

Glaze

Glaze tint

Combing object (can be a comb, a piece of corrugated cardboard, a steel-wool pad, a stiff metal brush, etc.)

Instructions

❖ Roll base-coat color over walls; let dry overnight.

❖ Mix tint with glaze and roll over a small section of wall, diagonally (crisscross strokes), not vertically.

❖ Drag combing object vertically down wall. (You can really use any pattern you want. You can zigzag or crisscross for a rougher finish.) Wipe object clean and drag next section of wall, redragging about a half inch of area just completed.

❖ Roll on more glaze, starting about a half inch into area just completed. Drag combing object through wet glaze; keep repeating until entire wall is completed. Move on to next wall.

Sponging

I gotta be honest with you here. The effect of sponging is beautiful, but it takes much longer to do than it looks like it should. If you like the look, but don't have the time and patience to complete the job, stick to smaller spaces like bathrooms or kitchens. If you plan to do an entire room, you've got to be really devoted.

Sponging also brings new life to old dressers, wood chairs, and mirror frames. The texture will cover any defects in the piece and the wide choice of colors will allow you to custom design a piece to fit a room. I especially like sponging the furniture in a child's room. You may have furniture that you think you need to get rid of. Don't. Try sponging it first and then decide. You may fall in love with it.

Supplies

Base-coat paint (you can use a flat paint, but semi-gloss will wear better in baths and kitchen)

Roller

Roller cover

Roller tray

Rubber gloves

Drop cloth

Sponge-paint colors (can use as many as you like)

Soft sponges

Instructions

❖ Roll base coat on walls, let dry overnight.

❖ Pour first sponge color into roller tray. Dip in sponge, wring out slightly, and then press sponge onto a piece of cardboard to remove excess. Begin in corner of room and press sponge randomly in one area. Redip sponge and continue until wall is finished.

❖ If you are using a second or third sponge color, wait until the first one dries and then repeat the technique with other colors. You can use different size sponges for a less patterned finish.

Washing

There are two ways to do washing: either wash the color on with a sponge or paint the color on with a roller and then wash it off with a rag. Washing-on works best for large surfaces like a wall; washing-off works best for trim. Doing both in the same room (washing-on walls, washing-off trim) looks terrific.

This is the easiest paint technique of all, even though other decorating books make it look like a herculean effort. It's so simple and so great-looking. The finished effect will make a room look like it has real plaster walls, a little weathered, like a Tuscan villa. The way I do it takes only about an hour to do a whole room (after base coat is applied and dried).

Supplies

Base-coat flat latex paint for washing-on

Base-coat semi-gloss latex for washing-off

Roller

Roller cover

Roller tray

Rubber gloves

Drop cloth

Paint for washing-on (flat) or -off (semi-gloss)

Big soft sponge (for washing-on)

Soft rags (for washing-off)

Instructions

❖ Roll on base coat; let dry overnight.

❖ Pour about one cup of paint into roller tray. Mix with about one cup of water (this amount will do an average-size room).

❖ For washing-on: Thoroughly wet sponge with paint, wring out excess, and then apply by "washing" the walls. Use big sweeping strokes. Some areas will retain more paint than others; don't worry, this is part of the effect. Wash until all paint is gone from sponge, redip, and continue until all walls are done. You can then go back and add more accents where needed.

❖ For washing-off: Roll paint on top of base coat in sections small enough to work while wet (about three feet wide, floor to ceiling is about right). Use soft rags to rub off as much of the paint as you want. Use the same big strokes to smudge and smear paint all over. You can go back and add to some spots if they need it later. Roll on more paint and continue until all walls (or trim) are done.

Brush-saving Trick

You can't always complete a paint project in one sitting, and washing out the brushes and roller is a pain. Do you throw them away and start over with new tomorrow? No! All you have to do is wrap the roller and brushes in plastic wrap or tinfoil (you don't even have to wash the paint out) and they will stay moist for a few days. ❖

Stenciling

Stenciling is adding decorative borders in paint around the top of the room, around door frames, to set off artwork, or just about anyplace you like the look. To do it use precut stencils (store-bought or homemade). Think beyond walls here; you can also stencil the backs of chairs, the frames of a mirror, dresser-drawer fronts, etc.

Supplies

Base-coat flat latex

Paint colors for stenciling (can be flat or semi-gloss or a sheer glaze)

Roller

Roller tray

Drop cloth

Gloves

Stencils

Spray adhesive or masking tape

Stencil brushes (these are stiff bristle, thin brushes)

Poster board for testing design and colors

Instructions

❖ Apply base coat with roller and let dry overnight.

❖ Use either spray adhesive or masking tape to hold stencil on poster board. Test colors by applying one at a time with stiff brushes. The technique for stenciling is to dip brush in paint, wipe off excess, and then kind of poke the cutout openings with paint. Don't brush on paint; if you do, some will inevitably slip under cutout.

❖ Once you've decided on colors, attach stencil to surface you want stenciled and paint. Remove stencil and attach at the next area you want to paint.

❖ If you want your stencil to have an aged look, rub it after paint dries with a piece of steel wool. Rub until paint begins to wear off a bit. Cover with a clear glaze. People won't know if it was done a hundred years ago or yesterday.

Chapter 7

Wallpaper . . .
and Other Stuff to
Put on Walls

If you love vibrant, dramatic walls as much as I do, and paint just isn't doing it for you, then you'll definitely want to consider wallpaper, custom-wood treatments, or fabric walls to transform your room. It takes a little more advance preparation and consideration because the cost and labor intensity is higher than paint (you won't want to rip out newly applied wallpaper if you hate it), but the finished effect can be worth the price. There are literally thousands of styles and textures of wallpaper to choose from, and another hundred ways to use it. Do you want plain paper, vinyl, flocked? Flat, glossy, embossed? Do you want to do an entire room, just above a chair rail, or only a border around the top of the room? These are all ideas to consider. Now is the time to look through magazines and decorating books to get a general idea of what you like. Take those pictures with you to the store—wallpaper is sold at hardware stores, paint stores, decorating stores, superstores—so you'll have a place to start. Before you go, read this whole chapter. When you're done, you might even know more about wallcoverings than the salesperson.

Types of Wallpaper

BEFORE YOU HEAD to the store, learn about all the different types of wallpaper and make sure you buy the right type for each room.

Borders

A wallpaper border is a roll of paper with a pattern on it that can be one inch to even twelve inches wide. It is usually hung all the way around a room at either just below the ceiling, eye level, or even just above a chair rail in a dining or living room. You might even use a border hung just below your kitchen cabinets.

Embossed

Embossed papers have a raised decorative surface that can be used as they are or painted over for a relief effect.

Flocked

Flocked wallpaper has a flat backing with a raised pattern. The raised pattern is then coated with tiny bits of soft material. Flocked paper is best for a dining or living room and not for a bathroom or kitchen because it cannot deflect moisture.

Hand-printed

Hand-printed papers are made by either silk screening or block printing. They are done one roll at a time (which adds to the cost) but the designs are unique and can be custom designed for you.

Heavy-duty vinyl

This kind of wallpaper is very thick and very durable. It is great for a kitchen or kid's bathroom because it deflects water and can be really scrubbed clean. You must use a stronger adhesive to hang it because the paper is so thick. If you don't like the super high-gloss finish, try regular vinyl.

Lining

Lining is used to cover walls that are damaged or bumpy. Wallpaper is then applied over the lining for a smooth finish.

Mural paper

Mural paper is actually a huge picture that is broken down into wallpaper rolls. There are murals of forests, children's book illustrations, the sky, just about anything.

Natural textures

Wallpapers made from natural fibers like linen, burlap, grass cloth or even nubby cottons bring beauty and texture to your walls. They are heavy and require strong adhesive, but have no complicated pattern to match.

Standard wallpaper

This category covers most wallpapers. It is thin, flat paper that comes in thousands of patterns, from flowers to stripes to abstract designs. It can be hung just about anywhere, but requires more care if hung in bathrooms or kitchens.

Vinyl

Used mostly in kitchens and bathrooms, this paper is resistant to moisture and can be cleaned with a sponge. There are many patterns available in vinyl; I have a great Laura Ashley print in my New York kitchen.

Selecting Wallpaper

THE PLACES YOU can use wallpaper are only as limited as your imagination. You can paper all four walls of a room, two, or just one. You can paint the lower portion of a wall and paper the top, separating the two with a chair rail. You only have to make sure the color and style go along with your basic furniture and accessories. Colors are easy to choose: They have to be one or more of your basics. The style depends upon the size and use of the room, your furniture, and the personality of the room. A large print needs a large space so that it doesn't overpower the room. You might use a large print in an Elegant or Classic room. If your room is Romantic, a smaller print or a thin striped paper is in order. A Modern paper might have a black-and-white geometric pattern. A Sporty or Southwestern room would look great with a natural fiber paper.

When you buy wallpaper, check to see if fabric in the same print is available. Think about where you might use the fabric. You can make pillows, a bedspread, a shower curtain, or even use it to cover a lamp shade. Even if you're not sure, buy a few yards (at least one) and decide later how you will use it, combined with the wallpaper to add those finishing touches to a room.

Also, buy an extra roll of wallpaper. Give the salesperson the dimensions of your room, and they will tell you how many rolls of that pattern you will need. Order an extra roll, and maybe you'll use it to cover electrical switchplates, the frame of a mirror, or a wastebasket, or umbrella stand. You might even take a simple box and cover it with paper to just set on a table as an accessory (you can use it to store coasters, a pad of paper and a pen, reading glasses, etc.). Do you have a card table that you use in that room? Cover the top with wallpaper and then apply a coat of lacquer over it. All of these extra touches will go a long way to add style to your room.

Don't just think about covering entire walls with wallpaper. Small doses can add big style for a fraction of the cost. I have a friend whose living room is all black and white. She has white furniture with black and white pillows, high-gloss black tables, and then she finished off the room by papering only the inside panels of a door with a black and white print. Even you can do that much wallpapering yourself.

The Right Tools for the Job

The first time I tried wallpapering was in a small apartment in Los Angeles. I was young, and I wanted to save money (like you're about to do), and I didn't have all of the right tools, so I borrowed a ladder from a neighbor. It was a little too small and a little too wobbly, but it was all I had, and I was anxious to get the job done. Needless to say, it was a mistake. As I climbed up to hang the first sheet, standing on the tippy top to reach the ceiling, I fell and broke about three ribs. After I got back from the emergency room, I went out and bought a new ladder. I should have done that in the first place; it would have been cheaper, and then I wouldn't have had the doctor's bill to pay. ❖

I have also seen people hang a big square of paper over a fireplace and frame it with decorative molding. It's like creating instant art until you can afford the real thing. You buy one roll of wallpaper (that doesn't cost much) and place a little here and there to tie everything together. And here's a terrific way to add style to your bookcases: Paper the wall in between the shelves. Just a glint of color will poke out above the books, but it will be enough to give the room a big dose of style.

Hanging Wallpaper

YOU CAN HIRE a professional—who charges about $17 to $25 per roll—or you can learn to hang wallpaper yourself. If you plan to paper a few rooms, it pays to acquire the tools and learn how. It's not that hard . . . I can do it. Stop laughing . . . really, I can do it. Really.

Get Ready . . .

The first thing you have to do is prepare the walls. If the walls are painted and flat, with no visible cracks, skip down a few paragraphs and go right to hanging paper. But if walls are lumpy, cracked, or uneven, start here.

Cracks: Wash walls thoroughly, then get out your putty knife and jar of all-purpose filler and get to work. Apply filler by scooping out a big glob and pushing it into crack. Scrape downward with flat end of putty knife to smooth. Apply a little more than you think you need because filler will shrink as it dries. You can then easily sand excess away.

Glossy Paint or Fresh Plaster: Apply a coat of sealant (sometimes called "sizing"). It roughs up walls a little to allow paper to adhere better.

Lumpy Walls: Apply lining over entire surface before applying wallpaper.

Old Wallpaper: It's okay (and sometimes better—if paper is over old plaster, removing it may pull down plaster) to paper over old paper if it is in good condition. If sections are bubbly, flaky, or torn, remove those sections and patch in pieces of lining paper. If seams are coming up, try to reglue them. If they stay down, paper over them (although don't place your new seams to line up with old ones). If they come right up the next day, you'll have to strip the paper from the wall and apply lining or sizing to walls before papering.

To strip old paper you will want to rent a steam machine from a tool rental store. It has a flat pad that you hold to the wall until the paper becomes loose enough to pull off. Use a wide putty knife to help scrape the paper off. You can also use a liquid wallpaper stripper product that you apply with a paintbrush, but believe me, a steam stripper is easier.

Get Set . . .

Before you plan your first foray into paperhanging, you'll need to get your supplies in order . . . who wants to run to the store in the middle of a project because you forgot an essential tool? Here's a list of what you need and what it's for:

❖ **Long table**—You will need some sort of flat surface to roll the paper out on, measure, and apply glue to the back. Two sawhorses and a piece of plywood will work fine, as will a picnic table covered with a vinyl tablecloth.

❖ **Ladder**—To reach ceiling and high walls.

❖ **Rubber gloves**—To protect your hands from glue.

❖ **Bucket**—To mix paste and to hold clean water for on-the-spot cleanup.

❖ **Wallpaper trough**—Sold in hardware stores, it's used for soaking prepasted paper.

❖ **Pasting brush**—A thick brush that spreads glue evenly. Get a smaller one as well, to do corners and to repaste seams if they pop up.

❖ **Scissors**—For cutting paper before it is hung.

❖ **Straight-edge knife**—For cutting paper around doors and windows after it is hung.

❖ **Level**—To make sure seams are straight when hanging paper on wall, and to use as a straightedge when marking paper to be cut.

❖ **Yardstick**—To measure the lengths.

❖ **Chalk line**—This will mark a straight line from ceiling to floor, showing you where to line up seams.

❖ **Paperhanging brush**—To flatten paper to wall without bubbles or sags after it is glued and hung.

❖ **Seam roller**—To apply pressure to seams to really seal them flat.

❖ **Drop cloth**—To catch glue and water spills.

❖ **Wallpaper paste**—For use on paper that is not prepasted. Can be powder or premixed.

❖ **Seam adhesive**—Extra-holding glue to really keep seams sealed down flat.

After you've assembled your tools, clean out the room or area you are papering. Carefully remove all light fixtures and outlet covers. If this is possible to do without damaging it, also remove wood moldings around doors and windows, and baseboards. This step is not necessary, but it makes trimming edges much easier.

Go!

Your wallpaper has arrived and you're ready to go. Before you start, carefully check each roll to make sure they all come from the same dye lot number. Different dye lots can be off by just a little, but it makes a difference and you'll see it immediately if you hang the paper without checking first. Open one roll and check to make sure that the pattern is properly printed. It's possible that the ink got smeared or the pattern is off-line. Once you've determined that the paper is okay, it's time to start hanging it. Give yourself plenty of time to work . . . it's a real hassle to have to stop and start all day long.

My first piece of advice is to corral a friend who has hung paper before and ask for his or her help. If you don't have one, don't despair . . . *you* can do this. I will give you basic instructions here, but there are a few videos and CD-ROMS on the market that can give you a visual education.

One last thing before you start: Probably

Do Over

It's so important to check your rolls of wallpaper when you get them. Most of the time, everything is fine, but if that one time the pattern is printed diagonally instead of vertically and you hang the paper—boy, will you be sorry. I made this mistake once. Thank God it was only a small bathroom, but I had to strip the brand-new paper (and of course, the store wouldn't take it back because I'd used it) and buy new. ❖

about halfway through hanging wallpaper you are going to say, "What have I done? Why am I doing this? Am I crazy?" You're going to want to give up, but don't. Take a deep breath and plunge back in. Focus on the great party you are going to give when your house is done, where everyone is going to say, "This is so brilliant . . . so creative . . . so . . . Martha."

Start Hanging

Here we go. Give yourself plenty of time and have a bottle of wine chilling in the fridge to celebrate when you're all done. Hanging paper takes patience, not skill.

❖ Most prints don't have to be centered in a room, but if you have a built-in bookcase or a fireplace, you will want to make sure that the pattern is centered over it, so start there and work out to the corners of the room. Measure the first sheet, leaving two inches at the top and bottom for trimming.

❖ Write "1" on the sheet and apply paste (skip if it's prepasted), fold it up, and place it in the trough to soak for about fifteen minutes, or follow the manufacturer's instructions. Cut a second sheet and write "2" on the back, apply paste, soak, and so on.

❖ While sheets are soaking (do about three at a time), hang the chalk line from the ceiling and snap a straight line on wall. Remove first sheet from trough and hang, starting from the ceiling (leave a two-inch overlap at top). Move edge to line up with chalk line and gently press edge all the way down to the floor.

❖ Use the paperhanging brush to flatten rest of paper (hold paper with one hand so it doesn't slide around) working out bubbles and creases. Once entire length of paper is attached to wall, use your utility knife to trim the top and bottom edges. Press flat.

❖ If your paper has a print, you must match the pattern of the first sheet to the second. Do so by loosely pressing second sheet to wall and then sliding it up or down until pattern matches. Use a level to check horizontal alignment. Once pattern is lined up, use the paperhanging brush to glue paper down, holding paper still with one hand. Trim top and bottom and then peel back seams about one inch and add a little extra glue to back of paper. Use seam roller to seal tight.

❖ When you get to the inside corner of two walls, try not to leave less than five inches to cover with paper. Thin strips of paper are likely to peel away from the wall, so if necessary, cut the sheet before the corner thinner. Also, don't make a seam in the corner: Wrap the first sheet into the corner, leaving about an inch to glue on the adjoining wall. Then align next sheet so seam overlaps and ends exactly at the corner.

❖ To do an outside corner, wrap the first sheet all the way around the corner and gently press down. Take second sheet and cover the first sheet, also wrapping the corner, and match the pattern. Use your utility knife to cut a straight edge along the outer corner from ceiling to floor. Gently pull up both sheet edges and remove the two excess strips you just cut. Apply a little more paste and roll corners to tightly seal.

❖ To paper around doors and windows, apply entire sheet right over openings and then use your utility knife to trim. (This is why it helps to remove moldings, straight edges won't matter so much because you will be covering them with the replaced molding.)

❖ To create an opening for light fixtures or outlets, lightly apply sheet right over them, press gently so you can see the outline, and then, using a pencil, draw area you need to cut out. Remove sheet, cut out, and reapply.

There, you've done it! You've added a splash to your room and saved a bundle in the process. Congratulations. Now, I'll bet you feel like you can do anything. You know what? You can.

Other Wallcoverings

WALLPAPER IS JUST ONE of many treatments you can apply to your walls to add style. There are a few others that you should consider. They can be used alone or in conjunction with wallpaper or decorative paint finishes.

Wainscotting

Wood paneling can be stunning. It can also really overpower a room. A good compromise is wainscotting, which is a series of panels that fit together vertically to create a half-wall of wood paneling. It is usually topped off by a chair rail or other decorative wood cap. If your house doesn't have wainscotting already, you can add it yourself cheaply and quickly. It comes premade with tongue-and-groove vertical connectors. It's sold at lumberyards or superstores, and all you need is some glue, a hammer, a saw, and finish nails to install it.

Wainscotting is most commonly used in dining rooms, with a chair rail and either painted or papered walls above. But I think it is great in any room, especially a family room or a child's room, because it's easy to clean and extremely durable. You can leave it natural wood or paint it to match your color scheme, depending on the personality of your room. I have wainscotting in my

New York bathroom. It's finished with a dark stain and a smooth finish for an Elegant look. A light pine wainscotting would look great in a Sporty/Country room. Paint it white or pink in a Romantic room. Try it.

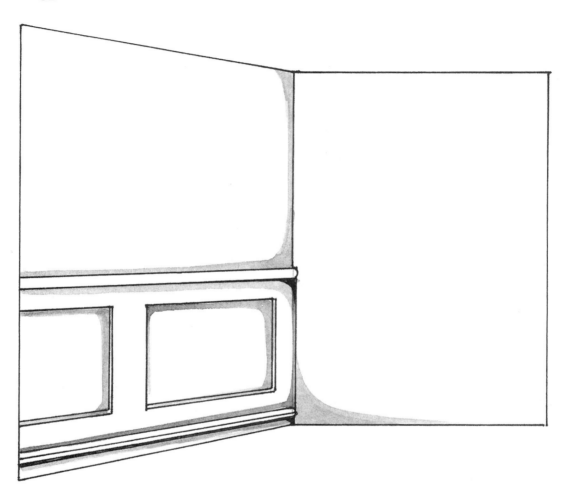

Wood Paneling

Wood paneling differs from wainscotting in that it covers the entire height of the wall. You can panel one wall or all four. You can leave it natural wood (great for a Southwestern or Country room), or you can use paint or stain to make it another design element in your room (use a rich red for a Classic room; a soft white for a Romantic one).

Wood paneling can be bought in huge sheets (four feet by eight feet) or it can be bought like wainscotting (tongue-and-groove strips). You can also buy faux wood paneling; it's plastic (making it cheaper and lighter) but no one will ever know the difference. In any case, you can install it yourself with just a few tools: glue, hammer, finish nails and a hand-held Skill saw (you can rent these) to cut vertical lines.

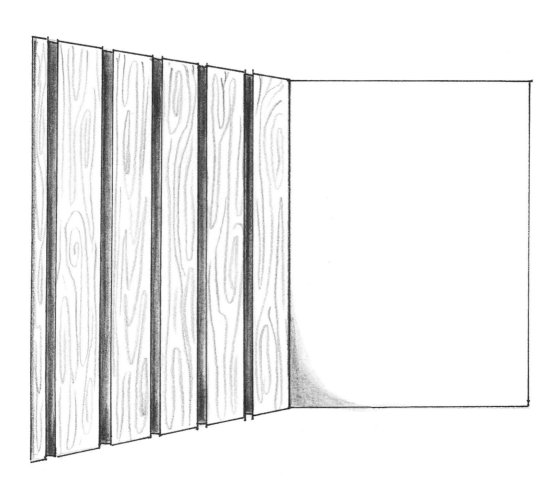

Fabric

An alternative to wallpaper is to hang fabric on your walls. I did it in my basement in Connecticut (it took all of two hours to do the entire room). You can do all four walls in a room or just two or even just part of one. You can hang it stretched tight or loosely draped or pleated. After you select your fabric you then will probably have to sew the panels together to create the width you need. Iron seams flat from the back and they will just about disappear.

To hang, you can go about it two ways. One, you can buy long, thin strips of wood and wrap fabric around the back and staple to hold. You make a sort of frame and then hang the whole thing on the wall; or two, you can staple fabric right onto the wall and then cover the staples with wood molding. You can even cover the molding with fabric, again using staples because they'll be hidden on the back after you hang the molding.

Another nice idea is to loosely drape fabric above your bed using the same fabric as the window treatments and your bedspread. You can use the wood-strip technique or maybe even use a curtain rod to create a fake window. You can make a fabric tent over your bed, too, by stapling the four corners of the fabric to the ceiling and letting the center drape down. Play around, see what works, but take some chances. You may discover something brand new.

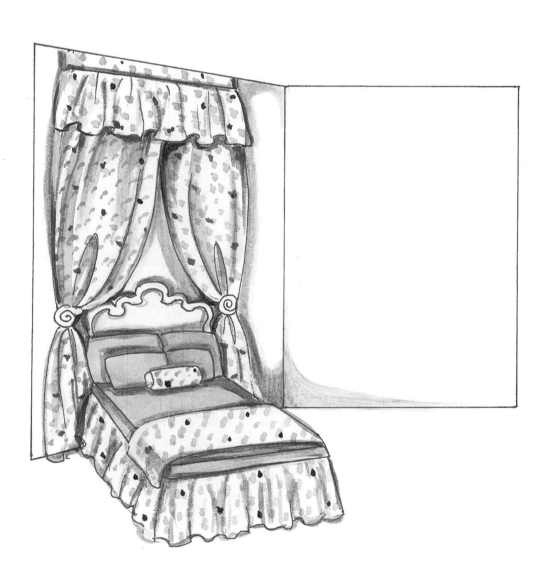

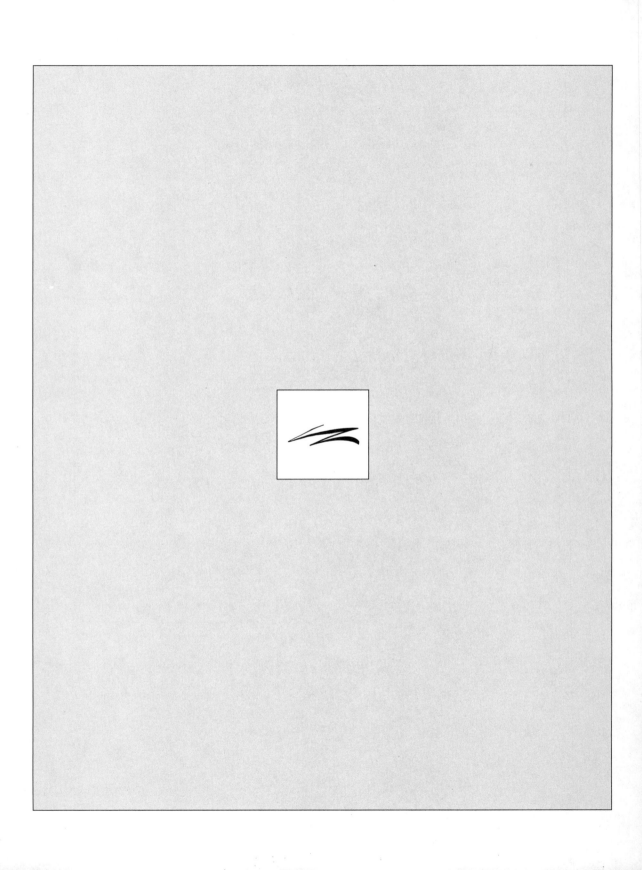

Chapter 8

Show Off Your Windows

Windows. Those big holes in your walls that are filled with glass. You can't pretend they don't exist and ignore them. They're there. They have to be dealt with. And they have to be dealt with when you are planning the design for a room. Here's your chance to be dramatic and creative and to show everyone your design savvy. Dressing windows (or "treating" them, as the pros call it) can be inexpensive and easy if you know what you're doing. What you can't do is nothing (unless that's part of the design and it would be in a Modern room). If you do nothing, it's too obvious that something is missing. You—and your guests—may not be able to immediately figure out why the room looks unfinished, you'll just know it does.

That doesn't mean that you must have intricate drapes or curtains on every window. There are lots and lots of choices here. You can either sew them yourself (yes, you), or order them ready-made. Professional custom-designed window treatments can cost tons, but, truly, you can find ways to achieve the same look by pulling them together yourself for a fraction of the cost. If you just can't make yourself learn to sew treatments from scratch, you can use store-bought curtains as your base and change them yourself for a more original look.

Window treatments are more than just a basic. Yes, they have to be functional. Large windows that face the street or your neighbor's yard must have treatments that provide some privacy. Window treatments in children's rooms must be easy to operate. But what makes them different is that they are an accessory. Sure, they must include one or more of your three basic colors, but the type and design also must suit the personality of your room. How do you know which treatment is right for your room? It's the same principle as you would use when dressing yourself. If your furniture is tailored (like a suit) you need to stick to tailored window treatments (would you wear a frilly scarf with your tailored suit?). If your room is done in all black and white Modern, your treatments have to follow the same spare lines. If you have yellow-and-blue-print French Provincial fabric on your furniture, you would choose fussier treatments like café curtains with contrasting-color button tabs. A Romantic room might have lace treatments; a Classic one, velvet floor-length drapes. It's a lot to think about. This may be a good project for a decorator. You can hire one by the hour just to help you learn about all the different styles you can consider, and then do the actual shopping yourself. Or you can have the decorator bring fabric samples, and then choose the style. Window treatments are real accessories (and, like accessories, you can change them with the seasons if you want). They will add the finishing touch to your room.

Out of Whack

A friend of mine lives in a New York apartment with small rooms. In the living room she has a petite couch, a side chair, and a few small tables. All of the furniture is sized in proportion to the small room. It was working fine. Then, she opened a design magazine and saw these sweeping, dramatic window treatments and duplicated them for her living room. Whew! When you walk into the room it's like a smack in the face. These drapes are so overwhelming that they make the room look like a cave. She should have chosen a simpler design to go with the size of the room. Just because you see something you love, it doesn't mean you can have it in any room you choose. It still has to be in proportion to the room. ❖

Learn the Terms

WHEN YOU'RE SHOPPING for window treatments, salespeople and decorators will speak in window code. They'll talk about balloon shades, valances, tiebacks, swags, and all kinds of other things you can't understand, let alone visualize. Here's a quick primer on what they're talking about.

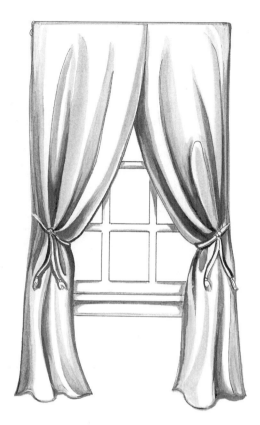

Drapes

These are long curtains, usually made from a heavy fabric, and are lined. They are pleated, and open and close by pulling a cord that runs across the top and down the side.

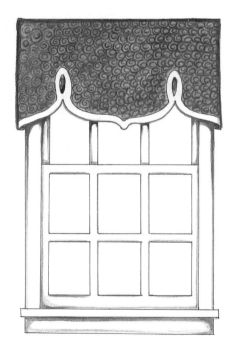

Valance

This is a short ornamental drapery placed across the top of a window. It's ornamental because it doesn't function to keep the sun out or provide privacy. It can be a wide, straight-edged piece of fabric or it can be thinner and scallop-edged. It is usually hung about four inches from the wall with curtains or shades hung behind it.

Café curtains

Usually used in a kitchen or bath, café curtains have two sections, top and bottom, which are hung on two poles. Each section can have one or two panels, depending upon their use. If you want to open them, use two, with tiebacks on the bottom set. They can have a sewn seam to thread a rod through, or they can have a straight edge, with fabric, metal, or wood rings.

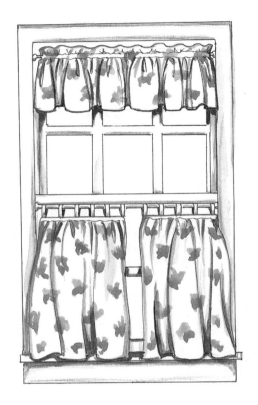

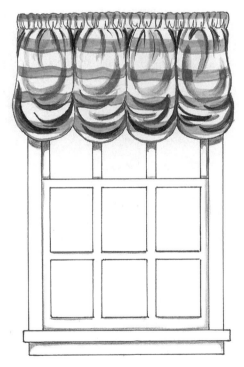

Balloon shades

When down, these shades look like a simple flat rectangle covering the window. When drawn, they are gathered into a series of puffy pockets created by inverted pleats in the fabric.

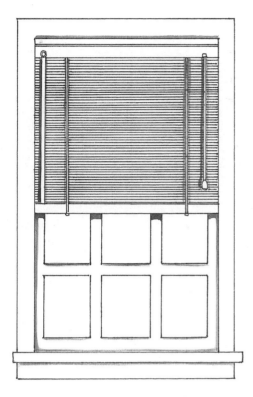

Mini-blinds

These are horizontal slats that are gathered and raised by pulling a cord, and opened and closed by twisting a hanging rod. They come in absolutely every color and size.

Vertical blinds

These are thick slats (usually about four inches wide) that hang vertically and open and close like drapes. They can be made from metal, plastic, or wood, or they can be covered in fabric to match your room.

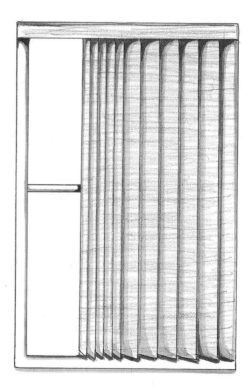

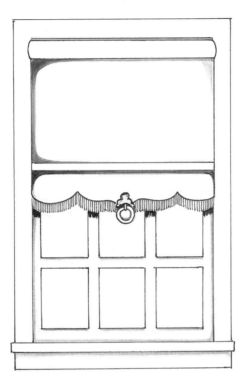

Roller shades

These are simple shades made from vinyl that roll up (often with a quick snap) when pulled. Usually used for privacy but when covered with fabric they can add style to a room. You can also have them custom made with scalloped or other style edges.

Duette shades

These shades look a bit like honeycombs. They're great for windows that have a small draft because they also serve to insulate. They are available in many colors and sizes and can be hung to cover skylights.

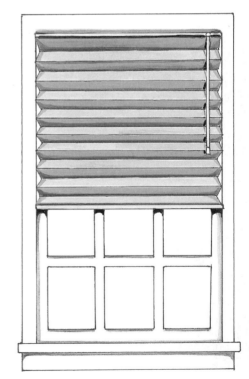

Swags

Swags are pieces of fabric (usually a rectangle) that are gathered and draped over the top of a window. Ends can finish at the top sides of windows or hang down the sides of windows.

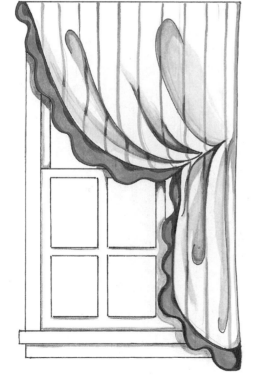

Reefed curtains

When closed, reefed curtains look like a softly pleated rectangle covering the window. They draw back invisibly by ring tape sewn on the drapery lining at an angle. A cord is threaded through the rings, which draws the curtains to the side without the use of tiebacks.

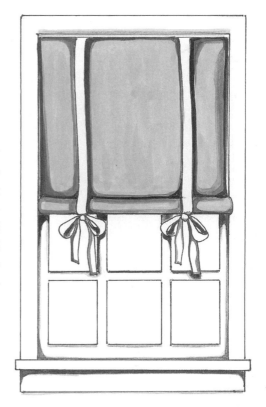

Stagecoach shades

These clever shades are so, so easy to make. They consist of a fabric rectangle (lined) with two ribbons sewn to the top corners and draped over the fabric, front and back. To open, simply roll up shade and tie ribbons in bows underneath to hold in place.

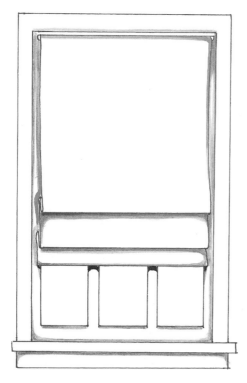

Roman Shades

When down, these shades look like a simple rectangle covering the window. When pulled up, the shade folds up under itself via two rows of rings sewn onto the back.

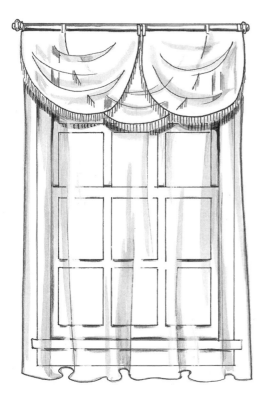

Sheers

This refers to the weight of the fabric not necessarily the style. Lightweight, almost see-through fabric may even be printed or embroidered (most common is white print on white fabric). They may have a straight seam at top or buttonholes for button tabs, rings, or other clever hooks to thread onto rods. Sheers may be used alone or under other window treatments.

Tiebacks

These are anything you use to pull curtains to the side and secure them there. You can wrap a piece of fabric (or fancy tassel) around curtains and attach to a hook on the wall or you can gather curtains and tuck them behind hook or other decorative ornament.

It's Curtains for You!

Y ou can hang lots of things on your windows, not just fabric intended for that purpose. I have a friend who bought six different antique coverlets and used clamp rings to hang them on her windows. They look amazing. You can use quilts, scarves, strings of beads, sheets, tablecloths, pieces of lace . . . Play around . . . anything can be curtains if you let it. ❖

Fun with Rods and Tiebacks

YOU CAN HANG your curtains on plastic rods and tie them back with simple hooks, but why would you, when there are so many decorative rods and tiebacks to choose from? With a little ingenuity, you can even make your own. You can be creative, even a little silly, and best of all not spend a fortune for a million-dollar look. Here are some ideas that I have come up with, but don't stop here. Come up with some of you own.

Rods & Finials

Standard curtain rods come in all lengths and widths. If you're not going to see them because they will be covered by the curtain seams, then go ahead and buy the least expensive ones you can find. (Unless you want decorative finials on the ends. Then you should look for rods that match your style in the room, because you'll see a bit of the ends.) If you will see the rods—because your curtains have button tabs, wood or metal rings—then try wood, steel, or wrought-iron rods. These can be found in many home design stores or ordered through catalogs like Pottery Barn, Crate & Barrel, This End Up, or Home Decorator's Collection (see Chapter Five: "Secrets to Shop With" for phone numbers). You can also use wood, metal, wrought iron, copper plumbing pipes, or even twisted tree branches from your yard as rods.

Plain curtain rods can be dressed up by adding decorative finials to them:

❖   Buy a stack of wood car wheels in various sizes from a craft store (they come in pairs, giving you a matched set for each end of the rod). Paint or stain them in the colors of your room. Glue them on the ends of rods—largest first, down to the smallest. You can do the same thing with wood napkin rings.

❖ For a nautical look, buy a wood rod, two Styrofoam craft balls, and a length of rope (a rope called Manila looks and works great). Scoop out a section of the ball to insert the rod into. Apply glue to the rod and attach to ball. Get out your sturdy hot-glue gun from your basic toolkit, and wrap the rod and ball in rope. Start at the center of the rod and work out to ball; tuck end of rope into end of ball. Repeat on other end.

❖ Use antique doorknobs on ends of rods. Buy wood rods that are at least one inch in diameter. Use an electric drill to drill a hole in each end. Pour in some wood glue and insert long, metal end of doorknob.

❖ You can add anything to plain rods that you can think of. Antique bottle stoppers, glass candleholders, Christmas ornaments, tassels, and toys are some ideas to try.

Rings

Drapes or curtains with buttonholes along the top cry out for decorative rings that are threaded through the rod to hang the curtains. If you buy store-made curtains, they may come with a set, but that doesn't mean you can't change them. If you have wood floors, match the wood rings to it. If you have blue walls, buy blue rings. Want a homey touch for your kitchen? Hang café curtains on wrought-iron rings.

One of the best ideas I've seen are rings with clamps on them. If you have fabric (even an antique quilt) that you want to use as curtains, you can attach the clamp without damaging the material. They're available from Home Decorator's Collection and Pottery Barn catalogs, among other places.

Tiebacks

Unless you want your curtains closed all of the time, you have to have some way of pulling them back and securing them. Decorative tiebacks do the job *and* add some style. Here are my ideas:

❖ Attach small hooks to the side of each window and buy lengths of rope with a tassel at each end (sold in decorating and fabric stores). Wrap around curtains and pull back to each side, so the tassel hangs in front.

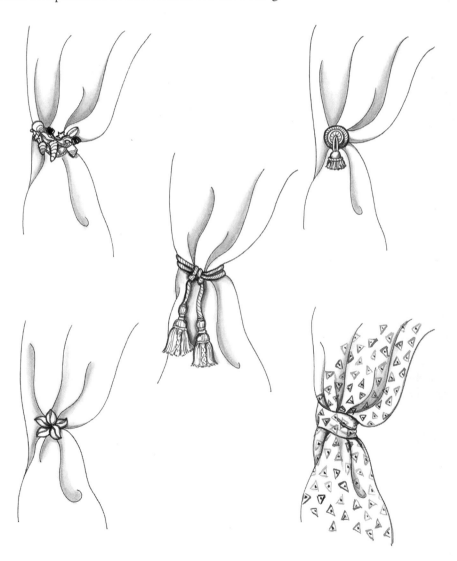

❖ Make or have made a fabric tieback in the same or a contrasting fabric. If your couch is blue with blue and yellow pillows, and your drapes are the same blue, make the tiebacks in the pillow fabric.

❖ Use antique coat hooks to tuck curtains over.

❖ Shop sewing stores for fun decorations—wide-width zigzag tape, fuzzy balls attached to a string, lace, ribbon, etc. Wrap them around curtains and pull back to hook on side.

❖ Buy tieback kits. They are hardware that you can attach to the wall and then attach anything you want to the other end. They are available at most home centers and through Decorative Window Accessories (781) 331–1319. Get creative. You can attach doorknobs, picture frames, pieces of wood or metal, a tile, anything you can think of.

Odd-shaped Windows

NOT ALL WINDOWS are perfect rectangles that easily accommodate traditional window treatments. Nor would you want them to be. Arched windows, picture windows, bay windows . . . all offer the chance to add drama to a room. In many cases the windows themselves are interesting enough to add style to your room, and so they don't need curtains or blinds. But if you need privacy or just feel that the window alone is too stark, here are some pointers on how to dress your odd-shaped windows.

Buy Extra Fabric

Anytime you buy fabric for decorating, buy an extra yard or two even if you aren't sure what to do with it. My friend's mother had lamp shades in her bedroom covered in her drapery fabric (you can do it yourself or go to a decorating store) and I can't tell you how fabulous it looks. I assumed a decorator had done it, but no, she and her hot-glue gun did. You can make matching pillows or chair sleeves. All for a small cost . . . but an expensive look. ❖

Arches

How can you add treatments to arch-top windows? Work with the curve, and you'll see how easy it is. These treatments may require sewing by you or someone else.

❖ Use a stiff piece of cardboard or wood to create a base for a fabric valance that follows the curve of the arch. Wrap valance fabric around base and secure on back (you can use staples; they won't be seen). Hang long sheers underneath and pull them back to right where the curve of the arch begins to head toward the floor.

❖ Use store-bought rectangle panels and thread them onto a flexible rod you can curve and fit into the arch opening. Overlap the curtains at the top and pull back right where the curve of the arch begins to head toward the floor.

❖ Have two hanging valances made (almost like two balloon shades) that will hang down to cover the top quarter of the window. Using either the same fabric or something sheer, make or have made two rectangle panels that hang underneath the valance. You can even make them longer than the window and allow extra fabric to drape on the floor.

❖ Use regular rectangle panels, but hang them over the arch (the top will be straight, as if the window were) and tie back right where the curve of the arch begins to head toward the floor.

Bays and Corner Windows

❖ Make or have made a series of balloon shades (two for each side window, three or four for the center) and hang them in a row. If you don't like the fluffy look of balloons, try a series of Roman shades.

Go Beyond Boring

My step-daughter has a lovely home. Her living room is done in all burgundy, sage green, and hints of tan. She chose plain tan balloon shades for her windows. They're fine, really, but a little uninteresting. If she went one step further and added a small valance or maybe long drapes in a contrasting fabric, her room would be so much more pulled together and dramatic. (Maybe I'll buy them for her. What a good Christmas gift—but don't tell her, okay?) I think she went the simple route because she was afraid of getting it wrong and it really does look okay the way it is. . . . But boy . . . the possibilities if you take a few chances. ❖

❖ Hang a valance that runs the full length of the window (for bays, you can either hang on the window—following the shape—or in a straight line on the wall in front of the window). Then, instead of hanging individual panels on each window, hang one at each inner corner (for a corner window, hang one panel in corner) and gather together and tie with a piece of fabric.

❖ Café curtains look great in bays and on corners, but get a little more creative by using interesting tiebacks or even alternate panels made from different fabrics.

❖ If you're adding window treatments to bays for color and style, not privacy, hang valance on straight wall above windows and then hang long panels down sides and tie back. If you don't plan to ever draw these drapes, you can use much less fabric or even an interesting shape like a scalloped edge.

Big Picture Windows

❖ Large windows usually face interesting scenery and may not need any treatment at all, but if yours faces the street or a neighbor's yard, you may need the privacy. Cut the window in half by hanging a valance along the top. Stay away from a straight edge (it will make the window too square). Try scalloped edges or points to add interest.

❖ If the valance adds enough privacy, stop there. If not, either hang full-length drapes underneath and tie back when not needed, or maybe vertical blinds in the same fabric as your couch.

❖ If you need only some style and not privacy, consider a long swag. The fabric could end near the top of the window, or you may want it to hang all the way down to the floor.

From Store-bought to Custom-made

If you already have perfectly fine curtains and don't see any reason to buy new ones, consider changing them . . . tweaking them . . . ever so slightly. My friend wanted to jazz up her daughter's room and didn't want to invest a lot. She already had plain white curtains that did the job. The room was soft lavender and pink prints, so she bought a length of one-inch-wide pink ribbon and sewed it along the edges and then used a piece of ribbon as a tieback. So simple . . . yet so beautiful. She could have also sponge painted the fabric in both lavender and pink, or added a valance in the same print, or hung pink shutters behind the plain white curtains. Look at all the possibilities. None of which cost a lot. ❖

❖ For a kitchen, you might use a valance and then a set of café curtains hung about halfway down the window frame.

Too Small Windows

❖ There's really only one trick to enlarge a too-small window, but it's a good one. Hang a valance about four inches above the window frame, but wide enough so that it covers the top of the window. Hang curtains underneath the valance, also starting about four inches wider than the window. This will create the illusion of a larger window.

Chapter 9

Underfoot

Floor coverings are a basic and yet they're not. You need them to walk on, play on, eat on. And they have to match your color scheme and style. But you can also use them as an accessory—yes, an accessory—to create an added bit of vavoom!

Flooring is a basic when you decide to keep whatever is there when you move in, because then you must start your design using the flooring color as one of your basic three (unless the flooring is wood, then you're free to choose three other colors for your room).

Flooring becomes an extra, or an accessory, when you can change it to suit your personal tastes. In that case, you may start with furnishings you already own and start the search for the perfect area rug, wall-to-wall carpeting, or tile to complement them. You might even install brand-new hardwood floors. All of these choices are available to you . . . and many more that you may not know about right now. But you will know what is out there, how to find it, buy it, and install it when you're through with this chapter. There's lots to learn . . .

Wall-to-Wall Carpeting

CHANCES ARE that at least one room in your home has wall-to-wall carpeting already installed. Unless it is hopelessly soiled, you should think about keeping it for now, because flooring can be one of the most expensive design changes you make. If you just don't like the look or feel of it, research and write down on your sample boards the kind of flooring you dream of someday having. For now, work with what you've got but hold on to your dream for later. One idea is to keep your wall-to-wall carpeting (even if it is stained, but not smelly) and cover most of it with a huge area rug. You save on installation costs and get the benefit of using the old carpet as extra padding.

If you are able to install new wall-to-wall carpeting, you're lucky—there are literally thousands of styles to choose from. Colors, patterns, textures . . . anything you can dream of, you can probably find. Where to start looking? Again, design and style magazines will give you your first peek at what you may want. If you see a photo of an Elegant room that you love, the wall-to-wall carpeting may be a warm off-white; in a Classic room it may be a rich green with small tan dots woven in; a Country room may well have a nubby Berber. Tear out the pages you like best for your sample boards and bring those to the store.

Carpet is available at stores devoted solely to it, or at hardware and superstores. Wall-to-wall carpet is sold by the square yard, with prices ranging from $10 all the way up to $100 per square yard. The price almost always includes padding and installation, but ask to be sure.

Carpet samples are either displayed on boards or come as individual pieces of carpet about two feet long. Most stores will let you sign out samples to take home. Do it. As a matter of fact, don't buy wall-to-wall carpet from a store that won't let you take samples home for a day or two.

Make your preliminary choices and then take them home to the room they are intended for. Lay them on the floor . . . and leave them there. Check them out in the daylight and with the lighting you plan to use in the room. Keep going back into the room. Squint. Make a little tunnel out of your hand and look through it. Go every half hour if you have to. This is what I do.

If the room isn't painted yet, lay paint chips on the carpet to see how they go together. If you are buying new furniture, add the fabric samples to your mix. When everything goes together the way you envision it, you're ready to purchase.

It will usually take anywhere from one to three weeks for your new carpet to arrive, so plan ahead for installation times. When you order the carpet, you will be asked for the room's measurements or an employee from the store will come to your house and measure for you. I prefer this for two reasons: One, I'll be a nervous wreck if they use my measurements, and two, then the store is responsible if they get it wrong. The amount of carpeting you need may not seem to make sense and here's why. A fifteen-foot by twenty-one-foot room would seem to need about thirty-five square yards of carpet (15 x 21=315 square feet divided by 9=35 square yards), but the store may say you need forty square yards. What's up? Carpets come in different widths—some are ten feet wide, some twelve, etc.—so you may need to order more length to patch in the width needed. And since you want the number of seams kept to a minimum, you will need more length unless you want to patch in two or three pieces to make up the gap. Are you following me? Don't worry about it, the store will order the right amount. I just don't want you to think you're being taken when they tell you that you will need more than you thought.

If you like the look of wall-to-wall carpet, but want to add just a bit more style, there are a few things you can do. You can create an outline for your room by buying two matching carpets and having a border cut into the main piece, so that the second color is about one foot inside the edge of the room. Choose a white carpet for a Modern room and have the insert made from a black carpet. For an Elegant or Classic room, you might choose a deep maroon main carpet and have the insert made in a deep tan.

You can have a piece of wall-to-wall carpet bound on the edges instead of having it permanently installed (the installation cost will be the same). You can use the same color binding for the edges or you can choose another one of your three colors for just that little extra bit of style. For a Southwest room you might try a burnt orange carpet with a green or brown binding. In a Romantic room try a rosy-hued floral print carpet and have the edges bound in rose.

If you have pieces of carpet left over after installation, you can also have those bound and use them for area rugs. You might use a piece as a runner in the kitchen (if it

Flooring on a Budget

Again, another example of resourcefulness . . . I know a girl who had no money, but a good mind for style. She collected carpet samples everywhere she went on the pretense of maybe buying new carpet (now, I don't suggest you do this, but use this story to jump-start your imagination); and when she had enough, she sewed them together and made a full-size rug. She did the same thing with little leftover bits of fabric. She sewed them together and made slipcovers. It was all a *Joseph and the Amazing Technicolor Dreamcoat* look, but it really worked. I wonder what ever happened to that rug? ❖

matches your color scheme) or as a doormat by the front door. If you have high-traffic areas, use an extra bound piece *over* your wall-to-wall to preserve your carpet. The area rug can be easily cleaned or replaced if needed. I always use left-over pieces inside closets.

One last word about buying wall-to-wall carpet: Ask the store if they sell remnants. I know, that sounds like you're getting second best, but really it's not. Remnants are the end pieces of big rolls of carpet. Someone else may have bought three-quarters of a roll of fabulous carpet and the store needs to find a buyer for the rest. The end of the roll is sitting in their warehouse, and they want to get rid of it so they lower the price. You come along looking for exactly that carpet and the size of your room is just right, and you can walk away with the deal of your life! The best part is that the whole carpet is there and you can roll it out and see how a big piece of it will look instead of just a little sample. I have almost always bought remnants for my homes; there's nothing wrong with it except you save a ton of money!

Can you install carpet yourself? Sure, but you won't save much money by doing it. Carpet is almost always priced with installation included, and it will take professionals about two hours per room. If you do it yourself, you will have to rent or buy equipment that you'll never use again. It will most likely take you all day to do a room, and it's just not worth it.

Seasonal Changes

I used to keep the same area rugs year-round, as I am sure most people do. A few years ago, I bought a sisal rug one summer for my living room. It cost about fifty bucks and was the easiest thing to clean. I loved it, but come winter I didn't feel as though it was cozy enough for the colder months. I rolled the sisal up and stood it in the back of my closet and rolled out the old wool rug I had kept. "Ah . . . that's it," I said. "I'll just change the rug with the seasons, and it's like getting a new room twice a year." ❖

Area Rugs

IF YOU HAVE gorgeous hardwood or painted floors, you may want to leave them bare or accent them with area rugs (this works well for every personality style). You can buy rugs or if you see a great piece of wall-to-wall, measure the amount you need and have it bound. There are so, so many choices. You can spend $50 or $5,000. You can buy rugs that you intend to replace every few years, or antique rugs that will last a lifetime. (Antique rugs are a great investment. They will hold their value or appreciate.) The quality you decide upon will probably be dependent on your family and how they use the rooms where the rugs will go. High-quality

Orientals may have to wait until the kids leave home, but you can buy less expensive copies now (as long as they are in subtle colors—bright, gaudy colors give the quality away), and no one but an expert will know the difference.

Area rugs can come in many forms, not just traditional wool. You can try sisal rugs (a natural fiber with a nubby texture), floor cloths (this is what I have in my New York dining room), or even painted canvas panels (you can buy canvas and paint it yourself). Just remember, rugs have to be in your three basic colors and work for the function of the room (you have to be able to clean them when needed).

Hardwood or Painted Floors

HARDWOOD FLOORS ARE the very best base for a room. Why? Because even if you choose to carpet over them, you know you have this gem right underneath that you can bare at any time. And also, hardwood floors are among the easiest to care for. If properly sealed, they are a cinch to keep clean; it takes only a quick swipe with a mop to clean them. If they get scratched, they can be sanded like new. Hardwood floors also go with just about any decor. If you have them, but perhaps they are too dark or maybe stained with red oak while you prefer white, they can be sanded down to the bare wood and restained and resealed. You can do this yourself by renting a commercial sander, but companies that do the whole shebang only charge about $1 per square foot and can do an entire house in about two days.

There are a few other options for hardwood floors: for a Romantic or an Elegant room, you can pickle them (this makes them look opaque white); for a Sporty or Modern personality room, you can paint them. You can do both these things yourself. There are special paints made for floors (ask at the hardware store) and sealants, like polyurethane (the new mixtures are water-based and dry quickly), to seal them. Sealants are available in either glossy or matte. Which one you use depends upon the style and era of your house. My house in Connecticut is from the eighteenth century, so I sealed my wood floors with a very dull-looking finish.

Cheap Transformation

I saw a friend's tiny apartment before she moved in, and I couldn't believe my friend was actually going to live there. It was so small and dark. I saw the same apartment a few months later and couldn't believe it. She had painted the floors a bright, pumpkiny orange. How jazzy was that? It was spectacular. She had the guts to go beyond the usual and turned a dingy apartment into a showplace. ❖

One of the nicest touches to a hardwood floor is to have a decorative wood pattern cut into the flooring around the edges of the room (great for a Classic dining room). Professionals charge about $10 to $40 a linear foot to do the job, but you can do it yourself if you have the patience.

Can you install hardwood floors yourself? You can and you will save a good amount of money by doing it. Flooring is sold in strips which have tongue and groove edges that easily slip together. They are held down by glue and finish nails. You will have to rent or buy a chop (also called "miter") saw, but this is a tool that you will use over and over again. You can buy oak or maple or walnut strips of flooring that are already sealed, or you can buy plain strips. I would buy the plain so that you can sand them after the entire floor is installed to smooth out any rough edges. You should be able to do a room in a day, with a second day for applying sealant and letting it dry.

Tile

CERAMIC, MARBLE, stone, terra-cotta, linoleum (tiles or full sheets) are all types of tile that each give their own unique look to a room. While kitchen and bath floors are the most obvious places to tile, that doesn't meant you can't also use tile in your living room, dining room, bedroom, or sun porch. Nothing is more stunning than an entire Modern living-room floor covered with bright white marble tile and enhanced with a few area rugs. (Of course, this is one of the more expensive options, but not completely out of reach if you wait for sales and do the installation yourself.) A terra-cotta floor in a Southwestern sun room is to die for. Faux marble green linoleum is an affordable option for an Elegant or Classic dining room. You see, you can get the look you want if you use a little ingenuity.

Tile is sold by the square foot. If you choose one-foot square tiles, you get one tile for the price; if you choose four-inch square tiles, you get four for the price listed. Floor tiles are usually anywhere from six inches square to fourteen inches square. If you need durability, go for the larger sizes; too much traffic over smaller tiles will cause them to loosen and crack (it also makes for more grout lines, meaning more spaces you'll have to clean).

While most tiles have to be applied with tile glue, there are a lot that you can buy that are called "press-and-peel." That means that they have the glue already applied to the backs, and you just remove the paper backing and press down. These tiles do not require grout. The colors and patterns of press-and-peel tile have greatly improved over the past few years, and the tiles themselves are made better than they used to be. You can even buy them in wood. Don't rule them out before you take a look.

Single-sheet pieces of linoleum have also come a long way. There are more choices now than the old industrial-looking gray speckled stuff. Linoleum comes in bright hues, classy patterns, and many textures. It's probably the least expensive "tile look" option out there. I should know, I have a faux green marble on my New York kitchen floor. Boy, is it easy to clean!

Can you install floor tile yourself? The answer to this question depends upon your patience level. Accurate measurements and precise cutting are required. You can definitely install press-and-peel tiles and linoleum sheets yourself (I have). Marble, ceramic, and terra-cotta may require a professional. If you do it yourself you will have to rent a wet-saw (about $35 a day) and take your time. If you ruin more tiles than you install, it might pay to get someone with more experience. But since it costs about $400 to install marble tile flooring in just a tiny bathroom, I'd say it's worth a try. It will take you a day to cut and glue down the tiles and another half-day to grout the lines. Make sure you ask the person you buy the tile from what kind of glue and grout are required for the type of tile you buy.

Checkered Past

When Frank and I bought our first country house in Ridgefield, Connecticut, we wanted to do something really unique with the floors. We ended up painting one floor in a black-and-white checkerboard pattern. Now, I don't have tons of time to sit around painting a floor, especially one with a pattern, but I was surprised at how quickly we did it (and how great it looked). Painting the floor cost us about one-tenth of what tiling would have, and we got a floor that expressed our style. I should have taken a picture because the people who bought the house took up that floor . . . it kills me. ❖

Unique Flooring

JUST BECAUSE everyone else has carpet or tile in their homes doesn't mean you have to. Broaden your options by considering unusual flooring. One of the best places to look is industrial-flooring catalogs. Ask the manager of your carpet store if they sell industrial flooring; most do. You'll see punched metal, thick rubber (some with little circles in it), maybe even Astroturf in a Sporty playroom.

The idea when decorating a house is to go beyond the usual and seek out something that suits *you*. Flooring is a great opportunity to express your style. Take advantage of the choices. It's like accessorizing a new suit. Don't be afraid . . . you *can* have something that is only yours and other people will say, "Wow! How did she do that?"

Chapter 10

Struck by Lighting

Before I met Frank, I thought lighting was lamps in each room, overhead lights in the kitchen, lights over the medicine cabinet in the bathroom, and, of course, lights that you flip on in each room (I never thought about where they were located) and that's about it. And if you're honest, you probably know exactly what I'm talking about. You have some lamps and you will use them wherever you need light. If you need more light, you'll buy a new lamp. But try to remember, the fixtures themselves are accessories and the lighting they provide is an integral part of how your rooms will feel.

Since I have learned how lighting can truly transform a room, I want to share with you some of the things Frank has taught me. But really, I just want you to start thinking about lighting in a new way. Think of it as creating a mood . . . a magic . . . an illusion. Let me show you what I mean . . .

Lamps

BY LAMPS I MEAN lamps with shades. They can, and should, be more than just white bases with white shades (although if you have a white room . . . boy, does that look great). This kind of lighting serves two purposes: to give you light where you need it and to give you an opportunity to use lamps as accessories. So lamps should follow your color scheme and be in one of your three colors. They can have fabric shades (how classy is that if your lamp shades match your drapes and pillows?) or parchment shades. They can be wood, metal, clear glass, stained glass. In a Classic room you might use small table lamps with a brass base and a Tiffany-style stained-glass shade; a Southwestern room would

have larger lamps, maybe with a brown wood base and a Navajo-print fabric shade; table lamps in a Modern home may be one-of-a-kind sculptures in a bright red with black shades that have very straight lines. As you can see, there's lots to think about here. Lots of choices.

All the lamps in the room don't necessarily have to match. When I was growing up everyone had two matching end tables on either side of a bed or sofa, and two matching table lamps. This is a rule meant to be broken. Of course, you can have two different lamps. They only have to match in size and style. You can have one ginger-jar lamp and one porcelain lamp. One shade can be a solid tan, the other a tan-and-green print. They have to work together, but they don't have to be twins. But do keep your table lamps in proportion to your tables. Use big lamps on big tables and small lamps on small tables.

And how about floor lamps? They are a great addition to any room (that is, any room where young children are not practicing their jump shots). It's a good way to get light without having to make the space for a table. Floor lamps come in all sizes and shapes, and all colors. In a Modern room, you might choose a floor lamp made in a geometric shape out of black enamel; in a Sporty room, you might choose a floor lamp with a wood pole and a rattan shade; in a Romantic room, try a floor lamp with a brass pole and a lace-covered shade.

Picture Lights

THIS IS a subtle way to create light and mood in a room. A picture light is a small rectangle or tube that hangs (or clips on) above your artwork. Its direct light will shine on your art and draw attention to it, and its indirect light will add

a little glow to that corner of the room. Picture lights are available in all finishes and colors, from brushed brass to shiny glass. They also come in different lengths for different-size pictures. They usually plug in, but some are battery-operated (these are easiest because then you don't have to worry about hiding the cord).

You know that boring light that is over your bathroom medicine cabinet? Why not replace it with a picture light? While you're at it, get rid of the medicine cabinet (you'll find another place for all it holds) and replace it with a terrific mirror.

Anyway, picture lights are in all my rooms. I have them over pictures (I had outlets installed behind them to hide the cord), and I have them at the base of walls just to add a little glow here and there. I've covered those cords with chrome or brass covers, which look great. I have five of these lights over pictures in my dining room alone. I flip them on, light a few candles, and I have the perfect lighting for a dinner party.

A Bulb of a Different Color

Put some time into selecting the color and wattage bulbs you'll use in your lamps. You want mood, but you don't want it to feel like a bordello (or maybe you do). A higher wattage is a brighter light, a lower one a softer light. Pinks will make you look better, yellows more sallow. Halogens are better for task work like reading or sewing. You might want a three-way bulb for a bedside lamp. Try a few before you settle on the final look. ❖

Floor Lights (Not Lamps)

Floor lights are also called "can lights," because they look like cans. They come in many finishes. I put white ones in light-colored rooms, or I have sponge-painted them to disappear in the room. I have also used black ones in darker-colored rooms.

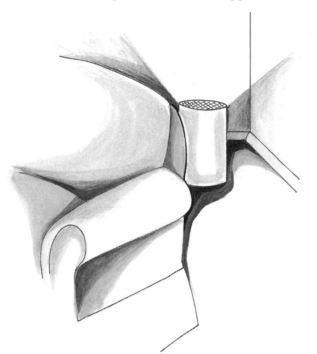

The point is to get the fixture to disappear and only see the light they give. Can lights project light upward onto the wall or ceiling. Frank really uses these lights to give a room warmth. He can have two to six cans in every room. I know it sounds like a lot, but I have to tell you, it really works . . . and you can buy them at Home Depot (really).

You would not use can lights for reading or providing the light you need to function in a room. They are strictly for style and mood. It's sort of like, *Hmmm, this room really looks great, but I can't figure out exactly what it is.* It's those can lights that make the difference.

Track Lighting

I USED TO THINK that track lighting was only for modern, stark spaces . . . but yet again, Frank showed me otherwise. You can use track lighting—and there are many, many kinds and finishes—everywhere, in every style of home. You can use it in the kitchen, in hallways, in bedrooms, in living rooms, anywhere you want to direct light to a specific spot, like a piece of art, or even against a wall for subtle lighting.

Tracks are usually hung from the ceiling or at just the top of the wall. You can hang a couple to provide reading light, or you can ring a room for a bright, explosive light. The heads on track lighting can be twisted to focus where you need the light. The heads themselves can be plain white, and will sort of disappear against the wall, or you can choose bright colors or metal or painted heads for a little touch of style. You can use spot or flood bulbs in track lighting, or small halogen bulbs for a whiter light.

Recessed lighting (the bulb is actually in the ceiling) will give you the same kind of direct light as track lighting, but the fixture and the bulb will be completely hidden. A bright bulb gives a big spot of light, but you can also use a low-wattage bulb or a colored one for a smaller effect.

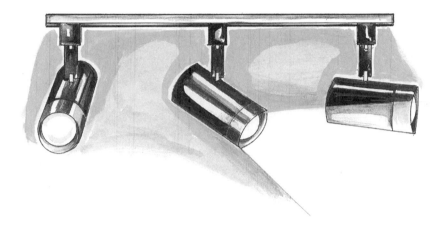

Bar Lights

THESE ARE MY favorite source of light. It's literally a bar with two to four small fixtures. You can put this light on top of a tall chest and direct the light toward a wall; you can use it on shelves to dance upon special objects; on tables behind a bowl or other object (the light just peeks out a bit)—really anywhere you need just a touch of light. Where does Frank find this stuff?

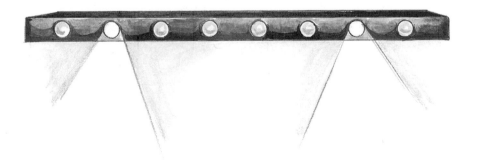

Framing Projector

THIS IS A LIGHT (either installed as recessed lighting or attached to a track) that directs light to one certain spot. A framing projector has little louvers that you can adjust to determine the area the light will focus on. They come in a square, rectangle, or circular shapes and differ from recessed lighting in that they create a very defined line where the light stops. They're expensive but worth it. Try it in your dining room. I have one installed in the ceiling above my table. When that is the only light on in the room . . . well, you can imagine the glow and magic it creates . . . it's like being in a movie.

Calling Doctor Lighting

I once went away to a friend of Frank's for the weekend. It was a wonderfully decorated home, but when we sat down for dinner, the host flipped a switch and a bank of four fluorescent lights burst on. I swear, I thought I was going to be taken in for surgery. We couldn't wait to finish eating and get out of that room. Bad lighting is so obvious. And you know something? It was the only thing I remember from that weekend. ❖

Under-Cabinet Lights

YOUR KITCHEN IS a place where you really need to see what you are doing. You need an overhead light or tracks for general lighting, but then you should place smaller lights under the upper cabinets for focused light. You can buy regular bar lights or, even better, buy light bars that have an adhesive backing . . . they stick right on and you can move them if you ever rearrange your kitchen work surfaces. Some come with fluorescent bulbs (softer light), some with regular bulbs (brightness depends upon wattage), and some with halogen bulbs (bright, white light). Have an electrician place new outlets close by so you don't have to deal with dangling cords.

I also use strip lights (it's really just a tubular bulb that plugs in) on top of a shelf but behind books or a vase. It's an intimate and uniform light that gives just a little glow. Another good way to use strip lights is to lay them on top of your kitchen cabinets (you can also use a string of Christmas tree lights for the same effect).

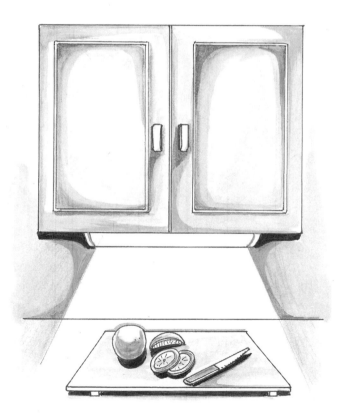

Sconces

THESE ARE LIGHT fixtures that attach to the wall, usually at just above head height (about six feet for those of you who are short!). Sconces provide little bursts of light in a specific location. Depending on the type of fixture you use, they will direct light up or out. You can install a group of them down a hallway, or just one to provide light over your favorite reading chair. Sconces are hard-wired into your electrical system and are usually turned on by a switch.

Planning Your Lighting

NOW THAT YOU know what everything is (look in the Glossary for more ideas), the first thing I want you to do is to make a lighting plan. Walk through each room and think about how you use the room and how you want it to look. These are two different things. You need light for reading, for preparing meals, to see. But you also need *lighting* to create the look of the room.

The second thing you should do is visit a number of lighting stores to familiarize yourself with what is out there. Walk through stores and flick on lamps, chandeliers, spots, track lights, etc. If you don't see the colors and sizes you need, ask. Often stores will have a display model and a catalog showing the lamp and its variations that can be ordered.

The third thing—this is when you know what you want—is to have an electrician come in and go over all of your lighting choices. You'll probably want to have some changes made: new outlets installed or moved (put in more than you need, you'll be glad later); hard wiring for track lights installed (this is so you don't have to run a cord up the wall; the track will cover the outlet); switches placed in convenient places (if you have a large room with two entrances, you'll want switches at both ends); and a dimmer switch placed in your dining room, etc. (I think dimmers are essential in every room because they can change the mood instantly.)

It pays to have the work done all at once, since electricians usually charge by the hour plus parts. Once he or she gets going, the work progresses fairly quickly, but if they have to come out and do one thing now, another next week, etc., they have to get all their tools together and get organized each time.

The most important thing you need to know about lighting is that you don't have to be stuck with the traditional table lamps and overhead bowls. You can go a step farther and let lighting give your home a mood. Since watching Frank at work, I too have expanded my horizons. I now have decorative night-light covers, small white Christmas lights strung around my patio, tiny little lights on shelves, and of course—the only pure light—loads of candles. Candles come in all colors and in sizes from itsy-bitsy to gigantic. Nothing is more charming or romantic than six or so together as a centerpiece. Don't forget to light them (I know people who never light their candles. They keep them for decor only. What good is that? Light them!) and have a wonderful evening.

Chapter 11

Your Living Room

In most homes or apartments, the front door opens right into the living room. It's the first room people see when they come into your home, so it has to make an impression. What do you want people to feel about you and your family? Do you want that first impression to be friendly . . . warm and cozy . . . dramatic . . . exciting . . . outrageous . . . chic? Let them see your sense of style.

The style of your living room can be anything you want—from Southwestern to Classic to Modern—anything . . . even an Eclectic mix of many styles. Your living room can be used as a family room if you don't have one, or it can be the one extra-special place in your home that is off-limits to kids and their toys. But this is not the important stuff. What counts is that you have followed the rules from the basics all the way through to lighting; you have created a room that works for all of its purposes. After all it's a room for living.

My Living Room

WHEN WE WERE renovating our apartment, Frank and I decided that we wanted a living room that we could use every day. We didn't want something with a "for guests only" feel. This was our home, and we needed a cozy place to relax at the end of a harried day. Since we also entertain frequently, we wanted the living room to feel dressy when we needed it to. We planned it so that when we are alone, we feel comfortable putting our feet up, and when we have guests, we have enough seating space and surfaces to put food and drinks on. Complicating these needs, was our desire to create a Classic room, since that's the style we love best. I think what we ended up with meets all of these goals. I know *we* love it.

When we decided to design a Classic room, we started with the pieces of furniture we already owned. I couldn't justify going out and spending money on something like a new couch when the one we had was perfectly fine. We had purchased our sofa awhile ago, and while it is nothing special, it has good bones. By that, I mean the frame is made of sturdy hardwood and the cushions are firm and well-shaped. When you buy a new sofa look for those features, and you'll have a piece that will last a lifetime.

We decided our colors for this room would be a deep red, tan, and bits of olive green (to tie it into the dining room, where the dominant color is sage green). These colors are definitely Classic, and I knew I could then find accessories to complement them. We had red velvet slipcovers made first (and used some leftover fabric to make pillows with striped piping), and then had the paint mixed to match. After a year in the apartment, we came to the conclusion that this look was too dark for the summer months. I then had cream slipcovers made, which I put on when the warm weather arrives. A few years later, I hit upon the idea of swapping the rug from Oriental (winter) to a light tan sisal (summer). This change truly transforms the room.

One of the things to be conscious of when designing any room is a sense of balance. A room full of furniture all the same height is boring, dull even. When you look at the color photo of my living room, you'll notice that I have a tall English secretary in one corner, and a screen of almost the same height in another, and a tall palm tree in another. The large ship behind the sofa is yet another height, as are the lamps. Give some thought to this when you are arranging furniture; it makes a difference.

Classic

IF CLASSIC IS the style you are trying to achieve, I don't want you to feel that you can't do it unless you spend a fortune on antique furniture. You can buy wonderful reproductions of antique styles. You can even buy less expensive, simple wood furniture and fool everyone by the clever use of fabrics and accessories.

You can tell from the pictures of my living room that a Classic room has lots of warm colors and fabrics. As I've said before, fabric and paint are the easiest, cheapest ways to totally redo a room. You could take a simple sofa (like mine), two wing chairs you picked up at a garage sale, your grandmother's coffee and end tables, and a pair of jar lamps, and turn these odd pieces into a Classic living room by using fabric alone. If your sofa and chairs are in good shape and in fabrics that will work with the room, you're ahead of the game. If not, investing in a set of slipcovers will pay off over the years. You might cover the sofa in a paisley pattern and the wing chairs in a solid color also present in the paisley. Make a few pillows from the solid-color fabric to throw on the sofa, and save another extra piece to use as tablecloths on the end tables. Choose another solid-color fabric for the drapes (perhaps a deeper or lighter shade of the color on the chairs), and make a few pillows from that fabric, too. In my living room, I have beige sheers under solid swags, but you might choose to make drapes from a print fabric with a solid color underneath, or hang a solid-color valance with print fabric panels underneath. You could then make fabric tiebacks from either the sofa or chair fabrics. Finish your basics transformation by painting your jar lamps in one of your colors and buying or making new lamp shades (maybe from a piece of your fabric).

Now that your basics are in place, begin to work on your groupings of accessories and artwork. Some ideas for a Classic living room are:

❖ Create a large picture out of eight small ones. Frank and I found a book of crests, tore the pages out, had them framed, and then we hung them very close together. (I used old *Vanity Fair* covers in my son-in-law's house.) This is a great solution if you need to fill a big wall and don't want to buy a massive picture. The benefit of grouping eight smaller pictures together is that someday you may want to separate them and hang them somewhere else, like along a hallway.

❖ Collect like objects. In my living room, in addition to the Classic look, I have an underlying theme of ships and things from the sea. The large ship behind the sofa ties into the grouping of shells on the center table, a plate with a ship on it, and an antique sea captain's watch.

❖ Create groupings of unusual items, like I have on the mantel. I have a fencer's mask, a rooster, a bird's nest, leather books, pictures, boxes . . . really they're all just stuff, but put them together and they create interest in an area. Their different textures and heights are what make the grouping looked balanced.

Elegant

I THINK OF an Elegant living room as one in a house without young children and for entertaining only, but it doesn't have to be. You can have chic-looking furniture and accessories and still provide the comfort needed for everyday use. Again, it is fabric that can make the difference (a little Scotch-Guarding goes a long way). To make an Elegant room more inviting, choose big, cushy couches and cover them in fabrics that are made to last, like thick brocades and tapestries. To keep the lines within the style, the cut of the slipcovers will need to be more tailored than the type you might buy for a Classic or Sporty room. The same goes for the drapes. They shouldn't be full of ruffles and fancy, curvy valances, but they can still be layered. You might use off-white sheers under heavy brocade drapes that are pulled back to one side and secured with a brass clip.

Flooring in an Elegant living room can be anything from white or deep green marble, to shiny hardwood, to lush, wall-to-wall carpet. It all depends on your three basic colors and how the room will be used. If the kids are going to eat dinner in there, I'd stay away from real Orientals or white carpet. If it's an adults-only room, you are limited only by your budget.

For accessories in this room try: a group of family photos in the same style frames (simple, not ornate); crystal liquor decanters; silver candlesticks; a solid mahogany screen; a grandfather clock; a faux-marble fireplace; white chenille throws; large mirrors (simply framed); and reproductions of famous paintings. Finish your Elegant room by buying fresh flowers weekly and arranging them in a beautiful crystal vase.

Sporty/Country/Southwestern

WHEN DONE RIGHT, this style of room is instantly appealing. You'll have to control your urges to pile accessories on too thick. You have to give them room to breathe; in other words, leave some space around your groupings so people can appreciate them. Other than that word to the wise, there are lots of options for a spectacular Sporty living room. You could use a sofa much like mine (either my winter or summer fabric would work), you could use a futon on a wood frame, a church pew with a fabric pad, a sectional in a white-and-blue mattress ticking, a reproduction Mission-style couch—the options are almost endless.

Color choices for a Sporty room might include blue/white/yellow (French country), burnt orange/brown/tan (Southwest), green/white/black (Florida and California cool). Fabrics would be cottons, thick muslins, brocades, and even tapestries if the pattern has a Sporty feel. Consider the same tricks of using matching fabric on tables, on pillows, and on curtains that I've talked about above and in Chapter Sixteen: Art & Stuff.

Flooring in a Sporty room could be terra-cotta tile, wide pine boards, or oak hardwood flooring. Cover these floors with area rugs—either one big one or a number of smaller ones (like I do in my winter-look bedroom).

Now the fun: accessories. There is so much that could go into this type of living room! That's why I warned you to take time and think it over. You could hang baskets; stack baskets on the floor or on tables; group pinecones and acorns around a selection of candles; group pieces of folk art; group driftwood and seashells; fill a vase with dried straw and flowers; lean a collection of antique rakes and garden tools in a corner; set up a checkerboard on a side table; use three stacked wooden hatboxes as an end table; or pile three huge pillows in great fabrics on the floor (they're art while no one's there and extra seating for a full house).

Modern

IF YOUR LIVING ROOM is small, a Modern decor can really open it up. If it's large, a Modern decor can be among the most dramatic designs. The trick, in both cases, is to find the middle ground between streamlined and empty. For this style to work, you'll want to keep the lines of the furniture straight rather than curvy, and the decorative touches simple rather than heavily ornamented. You are going for a light feel in this room, but you are still going to add pieces of your personality.

If you choose a Modern decor, it goes without saying that you like lots of black and white, and monochromatic rather than print fabrics. Since white is a given in a Modern room, you'll next have to decide how big a player you want black to be. If you choose it as a dominant color, then when you choose your third basic color you might opt for gray—for a quieter look—or red, royal blue, or kelly green to make a bigger splash. If you select black as an accent color, you can pick just about any other color to pair with white as your dominant tone.

Fabrics in a Modern room can range from muslins to leather. (This is actually a great style to use if you have young children because the furniture and fabrics can be sturdier—although you'll have to steer away from sharp edges on tables and chairs.) To make the room cozier, you might start with a comfortable straight-backed sectional sofa. You might cover it in all-white leather, wide black-and-white striped cotton, or even a gold linen, if that's one of your colors. Then you could add chairs with chrome frames and black leather seats. You can find them at garage sales everywhere. The leather can be replaced if it's worn or if you need to change the color to fit your room.

Lighting in a Modern room needs to be bright and white, which calls for track lights, recessed lights, picture and strip lights, all filled with halogen bulbs. You might also buy some unique floor lamps with a chrome finish (uplighters look stunning). For direct reading light, try some chrome swing-arm lamps bracketing the sofa.

For tables, think beyond the usual four legs and a top. You could use a thick piece of glass held up by four lengths of plastic plumbing pipe painted black, a chrome trunk on wheels, or wood boxes sponge-painted or marbleized in black and white.

Flooring could be white-and-black checkerboard tile or pickled wood with area rugs or wall-to-wall carpeting. You might try a piece of wall-to-wall with a black center, a white border, and black binding. You could use red binding instead, if that is one of your colors; it will help tie the room together just that little bit more.

Romantic

A ROMANTIC LIVING ROOM will definitely be cozy, so choose your furniture and fabrics with that in mind. To make my living room more Romantic, I could leave the sofa, chairs, and walls the way they are and make my statement with window treatments and accessories alone. I would change the solid swags to florals and replace the sheer panels with lace ones. (A great trick to infuse a room with Romance is to break up the room with a curtain, especially if your living room and dining room are really one big room. Hang a rod where you want the division to be, hang the curtain panels and tie them back with a satin tassel. You could even add a valance if you want). I would make new pillows from the extra drapery fabric and add ruffles to the edges. I'd replace the two heavy lamps with lighter ones, maybe wrought-iron or Tiffany-style.

I'd use a piece of fabric to hang over the edges of the coffee table, and on it I'd group a collection of antique linen napkins tied with a satin ribbon, pink candles, a few small china heart boxes, and a little bowl of rose potpourri. I'd replace my crest prints with a huge mirror in a gilded frame. I'd replace the picture over the fireplace with a black-and-white photo of my great-grandmother (if I didn't have one, I'd buy one of someone *else's* grandmother).

To bring interest to the mantel, I'd first drape it with a lace runner (you can pick up antique tablecloths and runners for nothing at garage sales and flea markets) and then cram it with lots of family photos in silvery frames.

The last thing I would do to create a Romantic feel in my living room would be to sponge-paint my sisal rug in reds and pinks and tans. This is a great trick. Sisals cost around $50, and you can paint anything on them. You can splatter them, do stripes, make a border, or if you are really creative, paint a mural on them.

Eclectic

THE ECLECTIC ROOM is the easiest to do and the hardest. Easiest because you can redo the furniture you have to fit any style; and the hardest because you are in danger of having no style at all. You absolutely must select your colors for this style room first, before you think about anything else. Your colors will give you the first clue to where you are going. It won't matter what pattern fabrics you choose—if you stick with the basic three. Use the same techniques described above when deciding where to use your fabric. Make pillows, tie in the window treatments, have a throw made, etc.

Once your room is painted or papered and all of your fabrics are in place, you can begin to bring in the accessories that will give the room its feel. For an Eclectic room, that could be anything, even a huge empty picture frame hung on wall or leaned against it. Turn to Chapter Sixteen: Art & Stuff and choose some of those ideas for adding groupings and other accessories.

Chapter 12

Your Dining Room

Τhis is the room in your home most likely to be ignored. When I was growing up, families ate dinner together every night. In the dining room. These days everyone's schedule is busy, busy, busy. The kids probably eat at a counter in the kitchen, and you might be guilty of occasionally gulping down a bowl of cereal, standing over the kitchen sink. I know you can't help it—it's just life in the nineties. But you can still make sure that you have a dining room worthy of a fine dinner every now and then. And who knows, if the room is inviting enough, you may even begin to use it every day. You may even start serving hot dogs and chicken nuggets on your fine china.

My Dining Room

MY DINING ROOM may differ from yours in one way: It also serves as a hallway to the kitchen, the back office, and the powder room. I have to walk through this room a lot, so it's important to me that it gives me pleasure when I see it (because I see it so much). Also, I don't have an eat-in kitchen, so we eat every meal here. What that means is that it has to be practical as well as stylish.

I have a Classic Regency table, but the finish is as hard as steel. It can really take a beating without scratching or staining.

The one piece in my dining room that might make you stop and say, "What is *that* doing here?" is the modern burgundy lacquered sideboard. It began its life as a TV and stereo cabinet. It's such a great piece that I couldn't bear to part with it, so I made it the beginnings of my dining room when we moved to this house. I chose fabrics that had hints of the same deep burgundy and collected a grouping on top that makes everyone believe it's a Classic piece.

While the overall look of the room is Classic, just like the rest of the house, the separate components are really Eclectic. The table is Regency, the chairs Chippendale, the floor cloth Country, and the plant stand is very, very Modern. Some pieces are old, like the wall clock, and some pieces are new made to look old, like the fabric screen that hides my air conditioner.

We used thick moldings at the top of the walls and around the windows to make the room feel cozier, and pleated Roman-type shades to add even more softness. The chandelier (which is electric, but could have held candles) is so beautiful that it almost functions like a piece of art. All of these elements on their own could have taken the room in any direction, but together they really do say Classic.

Classic

HOW DO YOU GET a Classic dining room without buying everything new? Suppose you have a Parsons table or a pine Country table? Paint them black. Or dark green. Or dark red. Keep a tablecloth (a paisley, a tapestry, a brocade) on top all of the time to hide most of the table, allowing only the legs to show. Are your chairs equally period inappropriate? Have slipcovers made, like I did for my summer look. I bought fabric at a discount shop for about $2 a yard, and took it to a seamstress who made up the slipcovers for about a tenth of the price of new chairs.

To really make the furniture disappear (if it's not truly Classic), you need to divert the eye elsewhere. Put up a chair rail and wallpaper from there to the ceiling. Choose a small print, maybe seashells, little bouquets of flowers, or leaves. If you select a print such as miniature sailing schooners, you could turn it into a theme for the room and then choose other accessories to fit that mold.

Another inexpensive trick to turn a so-so room into a showstopper is to change the texture of the walls and doors by adding molding. In a Classic dining room, you could apply rectangular strips of molding to doors (I did a rect-

My living room has a Classic feel, but it is really Eclectic: The chairs, the painting above the fireplace, and the screen are definitely Classic, but the cocktail table is Modern and the sisal rug has more of a Sporty quality. But I think it all works together. What do you think?

PHOTOGRAPH BY TRIA GIOVAN

I love rich colors, and the red velvet sofa, needlepoint chair, paisley pillows, animal-print throw, and Oriental rug really do the trick here in my living room. I reupholstered the old sofa first and *then* had the paint mixed to match. It would never have worked the other way around.

PHOTOGRAPH BY TRIA GIOVAN

Same living room, same furniture—I just added cream-colored slipcovers (they really didn't cost that much to have made) and changed the accessories, and it really transforms the room. That's the secret of successful decorating!

Accessories

really add your personal style to a room, and they don't have to be that complicated or expensive. See that watch—it only cost me $50 at a flea market. It doesn't work, but who cares—it's the look that counts.

Just like

getting dressed, my favorite part of decorating is finding the right accessories. I really love collecting interesting, unusual "stuff" to add that finishing touch. And you never know where you might find it— that bird's nest (it's real!) was just lying on the grass by my Connecticut home.

PHOTOGRAPH BY TRIA GIOVAN

I don't have an eat-in kitchen, so my dining room needs to be comfortable enough for everyday use. I use the cream slipcovers in the summer; they're made out of the same material as the ones in the living room. Also, notice the seashells and the candles. See how this room looks different than the living room, but it's all tied together by the accessories.

Remove the slipcovers, change the table setting, and— Voilà! A new look.

PHOTOGRAPH BY TRIA GIOVAN

I love this sideboard—okay, it's not really a sideboard; it used to be a TV and stereo cabinet. But with the right accessories, this lacquered piece of furniture works in my Classic dining room.

Would you believe

this is a cheap folding table I bought at a discount store? By draping it with fabric and grouping some great pieces on top, I've created a dramatic entranceway. Quite impressive, if I do say so myself.

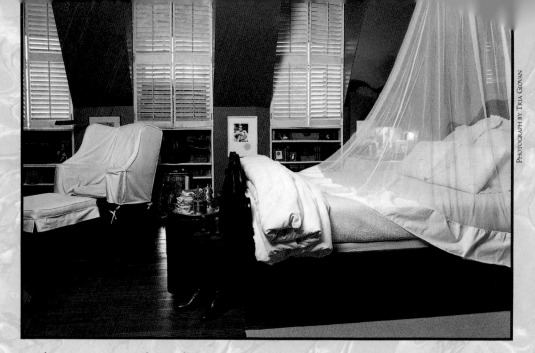

PHOTOGRAPH BY TRIA GIOVAN

I love my bedroom, and you should love yours—it should be your spe-

cial place. In the summer, I hang sheer mosquito netting over the bed to give it a Romantic feel. No matter what style room you have—Classic, Modern, or Sporty—you definitely want a little romance in the bedroom!

In the winter, I go for darker colors in the bedroom. Do you notice how the screen

in the corner, the sheets, and the throw pillow on the chair share the same animal print? It's all about tying it all together.

PHOTOGRAPH BY TRIA GIOVAN

A saddle in the bedroom? Yes, it works! I was going for an equestrian theme (notice the prints and the boots by the side of the bed in the previous picture). If you pick one concept and group like items, you're going to wind up with a room that screams with style.

Hannah's room is

feminine, but not childish. This look will still work when she's a teenager.

Frank and I bought our granddaughter Hannah an unfinished wood dresser and then hired an artist to paint it. You could probably do this yourself. No artistic talent? Sponge-paint it, stencil it, or have your child paint it for a look that's one-of-a-kind.

angle and a square on mine, but you could even do six rectangles stacked two-by-two) to create a raised panel look. Paint them the same color as the door so it looks like the real thing. I've suggested putting up chair rails for this style room (they function to keep the walls from getting scratched when you lean chairs against them) because they add a design element common in older houses. They also give you a more interesting surface on the wall. One last thing you can do with molding is to use it as shelving to place prints or photos on. You can buy wider widths and place one of your collections—like cups and saucers—on it. Buy lengths of molding at lumberyards and finish them yourself, or order shelf-size pieces from a catalog (one is Hold Everything, 800–421–2264).

Elegant

AS WITH THE living room, when I think of an Elegant dining room, I think of one used by adults and for special occasions only. I think of a fancy dining-room set with all matching pieces. Maybe a burl wood table with inlays, wood chairs with upholstered seats, a matching beveled glass–front china cabinet and sideboard. I think of hardwood or marble floors with an Oriental rug over it. I think of a crystal chandelier that takes a whole day to clean. Boy, it sounds like you have to have a million bucks to pull this room off!

It does, if you buy the very best of all the pieces above. But you can probably pull off an Elegant look by cutting corners, where you can get away with it, and using the right colors and fabrics. One of the things I have discovered is that used furniture is cheap. Really cheap. It doesn't mean it's lousy, just that some person with a million bucks didn't want it anymore. I have found great bargains at auctions and used-furniture stores. I'm not talking about antiques here, but good, solid furniture in lasting styles. It may take some patience and lots of searching, but I know you can find a perfect using dining-room set out there. (One thing to remember: Don't buy the table without the chairs, because chairs bought separately are very expensive for some reason.)

Choose your colors by reviewing the ones in the living room, especially if the rooms are located close by. You may choose one color from the living-room palette and add two different ones for the dining room. (I actually used all of the same colors, but in the living room, I gave the red more importance and in the dining room, green is the dominant color.) For wallpaper, solids and thin stripes work best for an Elegant dining room. Stay away from florals and old-fashioned prints.

As for the flooring, there are plenty of stores (department stores even) that sell fine copies of Oriental rugs. If you already have hardwood floors, sand them down and buy a new rug. If you have tile or carpet (with plywood underneath), you can install new hardwood floors right over it. You can buy it at any home-improvement store and install it yourself. I know. I've done it.

The quality of the crystal is what determines the price of a chandelier. All crystal reflects light and twinkles. Really good crystal just twinkles a little more. It just doesn't matter that much. Buy what you can afford and enjoy it!

Sporty/Country/Southwestern

THIS STYLE IS fun to create for a dining room, because it allows you to bring in whimsical pieces. You chose this style because you like interesting things, and I encourage you to have fun with it. For instance, you might choose to build a banquette along one wall, set your table in front of it (this is great in a small room because when it's not in use, you can push the table up against the banquette), and use chairs on the other side. A sideboard might be a Parsons table draped with a piece of fabric. Instead of a china cabinet, use open shelves, maybe painted in three different colors. You could even hang an unusual mirror in this room, like the shell mirror I have in my dining room.

Country colors span a wide range, but nothing is more charming than the Provincial (French Country) palettes of yellow, blue, white and yellow, green, white. This region of France is well-known for it's fine restaurants and wineries. Why not bring that feeling to your home? Use one of the above palettes, but mix up the prints. Try a valance of one print (maybe small flowers) and the drapes underneath in another (stripes). Use another print for your seat cushions, and then tie everything together by using the seat fabric to make curtain tiebacks, and the valance print to make place mats. This would be so charming!

Flooring in this room can be wide pine boards, tile, hardwood with rag area rugs, or how about a hand-painted floor? You could make a checkerboard pattern (like my floor cloth) or wide stripes, or just do a border around the edges. The great thing about a hand-painted floor is that if you tire of it, just paint something new.

Lighting in a Country room could be a wrought-iron chandelier, a patina chandelier (it's a faux finish that mimics tarnished copper—think Statue of Liberty), a wood chandelier, or maybe a piece of folk art that you wire yourself. On the walls, I would try punched-tin sconces. I once went to a bed-and-breakfast that had these, and I thought they looked great. On closer inspection, I realized all they were were big food cans (institutional size) that the owners had hand-punched a design in. They were nailed to the wall over a single light bulb. Talk about creative . . . not to mention inexpensive!

Modern

YOUR TABLE WILL be the main focal point of this room, and you have a very wide choice. You could use a black Parsons table, a glass-topped table with round chrome legs, a white painted table with a square black pedestal underneath, a stainless steel table . . . any of these would be great. For chairs, the styles for a Modern room are the fully upholstered (even the legs) type, director's chairs, a more refined version of folding chairs, spindly café chairs in black wrought iron, or something in a unique and wonderful design that you discover on your own.

Sideboards and china cabinets should be in the same Modern style, but use a little creativity here. The fun of high tech is discovering new uses for regular objects. Put it into practice by maybe using a vertical CD holder tower to store plates. I know a woman who puts all of her silverware and table linens in a bright-red tool caddy (you know, those tall things auto mechanics use). Don't be afraid to turn the impractical into the practical in this room.

One of the dangers of designing any Modern room is making it too stark, too austere. You have to add the touches that will bring a little warmth in. Have black silhouettes made of all your family members, mount them individually on white mattes, and finish with a black frame. Hang these randomly or in a row from a piece of industrial-size metal cable. Create a fake window by first painting a square on the wall, then painting on a shade—pulled down—and then hang a curtain rod above with fabric drapes hanging down the sides. Run a length of glass shelving all the way along one wall and fill it with groupings of candles, photos, vases (buy flowers), and other interesting items. Place a few strips of bar lighting on it . . . and wow . . . you've made a statement.

The last area you must pay attention to is the lighting. You can use track or recessed lights, framing projectors, uplighters in the corners (or behind a plant), can lights, and—for real drama—a pendant lamp over the table. I have seen pendant lamps in all shapes and sizes. You can buy one for this Modern room that looks a little like the planet Saturn, or one that has a simple cone shape (three of these together look fantastic), or try a pendant lamp that is nothing more than a chrome rod hung horizontally with mini track lights in it.

Romantic

DINNER FOR TWO. Dinner for eight. You love both. So you need to create a cozy place, yet have enough of the "stuff" to accommodate your guests. You can start with just about any style furniture because it really is, more than most style rooms, the fabric and paint that will transform your dining room into a haven of love.

If you want to do something special, apply a white chair rail and sponge-paint the lower portion of the walls in white, soft pink, and pale, pale yellow. Wallpaper the top portion of the walls in a tiny floral print in those same colors. Attach a white strip of molding at the top of the walls. Keep going . . . paint your dining-room table and chairs. Paint the table white and then either sponge-paint it to match the walls or paint a stencil pattern around the edges and down the legs. Do the same for the chairs (I've seen chairs with sayings painted on them. You could do the same. *How do I love thee* . . .). (Just a note: You don't always have to use pink for a Romantic room, but stick to pastels.)

On the windows, hang a solid-color valance with curvy edges. Underneath, hang rectangular lace panels, tied back with the solid-color fabric used in the valance. Have shades made in the same fabric as the wallpaper to complete the look. Balloon shades are another option here, because they give the layered look you're going for. To really complete this room, make chair cushions from the same fabric as the wallpaper. Whew! A lot of work, but worth it.

For lighting in a Romantic room, think soft. You could use a chandelier much like mine and then use as many candles as you can. Sit them on shelves, on little tables, on the main table. A great centerpiece for a Romantic room is a bowl of floating flowers and candles, set on a lovely piece of antique lace. The important thing about candles is that you have to light them. Even if you never use them, light them at least once so it looks as though you do.

Eclectic

IF YOU ARE starting with a mishmash of furniture, the style of your dining room will most likely be Eclectic. Just like in the living room, choose your colors very carefully and stick to them when choosing everything from fabric to paint to flooring. It's so, so important here.

Say you inherited Grandma's dining-room set. It's some funny wood that is a color of brown you can't really name. The legs of the table are intricately carved, as is the front of the china cabinet. Add to that the fact that your dining room is paneled in that brown plastic stuff that people used to have in something called a "rumpus" room. The only bonus so far is that you pulled up the Harvest Gold carpet and found unmarred hardwood floors underneath. What do you do?

There are lots of ways you could go. One would be to get a lot of paint supplies and go to work. First, paint the wood paneling in one of your colors—let's say yellow, because you are sort of leaning toward a Southwestern look. Next, paint all of the wood furniture in warm, orange terra-cotta. Replace all of the drawer pulls and handles on the china cabinet with yellow porcelain ones. Buy an inexpensive sisal rug and in rusty brown, paint a border about six inches from the edge. Sand and refinish the wood floors with a dark stain (to match the brown in the rug). We're almost there. . . . Look around for fabrics in your colors. They could be monochromatic or stripes or patterns, whatever you like. Make or buy matching curtains and seat cushions. There, you've taken all the wrong pieces, and put them together. You've hardly spent anything, and your dining room looks great, doesn't it?

Finish your room with things like a big mirror leaning against a wall, a row of cowboy hats hung on pegs, a shelf of topiary plants, a giant floor urn filled with pussy willows, a wall clock (or how about five hung in a grouping?), a tea cart filled with baskets and candles . . . all the things that give a room it's real personality.

Chapter 13

Your Bedrooms

There are bedrooms and then there is the master bedroom. While you want the other bedrooms in your house to be stylish, the master bedroom—yours—is the one that really matters. It's the one place in the house that is for you and your husband alone to enjoy. It's your private place where it's fair to say, "No visitors allowed." So it's important that you get the mood right in the master bedroom. You need to feel cozy, sexy, and loved in here (this isn't a place for clutter; get organized!) so that you have a place to recharge your batteries.

While you need a bed, of course, and other furniture, this may be the room where you display your most treasured items. Special lamps, your collection of miniatures, framed postcards from romantic trips . . . you know, things that bring the two of you together . . . and better yet . . . things you don't want to share with anyone but him. In other words . . . if you build it right, romance will come.

My Bedroom

THE STYLE OF MY bedroom is really Eclectic, but I used accessories that give it the same Classic feel as the rest of the apartment. You can see from the pictures in the color insert that the architecture in my bedroom is Modern (the windows have square edges with no casings). I chose to use Plantation shutters on the windows and simple shelving below to bring more of an old-world feel into the room. For a Country look, I would have used stagecoach or balloon shades; for a Modern look I might have used chrome or copper mini-blinds. You can see how even those small changes would give the room a completely different feel.

I also applied a narrow wallpaper border around the top of the room to break up the open feel of the ceiling. I used a green, red, and tan paisley, because that is period appropriate, but you could just as easily use a bold geometric print border for a Modern room or a floral print border for a Sporty or Romantic room.

Just like in my living room, I have different summer and winter versions of my bedroom. In the winter, I prefer darker, richer, warmer colors and textures; and in the summer, I like the whiter, airier version. The only things I change are the linens and the rugs (you'll also notice I turn around the animal-print screen in the summer and use the reverse side as a backdrop for the same grouping). For winter, I use paisleys, animal prints, and velvety fabrics; for the summer, I go with all creamy tones and lighter fabrics. I also change the rugs from lots of Oriental area rugs in winter to a single tan sisal in the summer.

Classic

SINCE MY BEDROOM is Classic, one look at the pictures should give you ideas for the way such a room might look. While a wood bed seems integral to a Classic design, that's not true. You could use a brass bed or a bed you have painted in a faux marble. If you already have a platform bed and don't want to replace it, something as simple as adding padded fabric sides (you can do this yourself by just using a layer of quilt batting and stapling the fabric over it, hiding staples on the back) will transform the bed into a new piece of furniture. Use some of the same fabric to make pillows and curtains. You might even have a lamp shade made to match.

I am telling you, and I think I've said it about fifty times in this book, you can use fabric anywhere in your house to completely change its look. You really want to experiment with fabric in a Classic home, because if you rely on furniture alone, it will cost you a fortune. One thing you could do in a Classic bedroom is to make round circles out of plywood, set them on a short pedestal (or even a pile of big books), cover them with fabric that matches your pillows, and instantly you have inexpensive bedside tables. You could even use two different styles of fabric, as long as they contain the same colors. You might also make a fabric door for your master bathroom. If total privacy isn't an issue, remove the door and run a curtain rod at the top of the door frame and hang a simple rectangular curtain panel. At a fabric store, find a really great length of silk rope with a tassel to tie it back with, and you've got a great Classic look.

This type of bedroom is sort of fussy, with little groupings here, mirrors there, maybe a cedar chest to hold blankets, a screen . . . stuff. Create your bedroom groupings much like you did in other parts of the house (see Chapter Sixteen: Art & Stuff for more ideas). You might reserve a special place for things that you really don't want anyone else to touch, like miniature crystal animals or framed photographs of your great-grandmother. This is *your* room.

The last thing you might have to deal with in a Classic room is the fact that most of us now have a TV and VCR in our bedroom. It looks so out of place in a room you are trying to infuse with old-world charm. What I do in my bedroom is hide all of my electronics behind a cheval mirror. You flip up the mirror to watch, flip it down to hide the TV. The other thing I have done is buy leather cases for my videotapes (we have so many!). I stack them on shelves and they look like old books. Just another trick to show your design savvy.

Elegant

THERE ARE LOTS of ways you can go to create an Elegant bedroom. You could have white marble floors, tailored damask drapes, a custom-built, sleek wall unit . . . you could have highly polished wood floors, simple floral drapes with blinds behind them, antique armoires . . . you could have a creamy wall-to-wall carpet, rose-and-cream Roman shades, lacquered dressers. There are many, many versions of an Elegant bedroom, but what they all have in common is a simplicity, along with a rich look (even if it's a fake rich look). You'll see spare lines, lush fabrics—you know, the good stuff.

While the big stuff may have a "don't touch me" quality, the little stuff should fit your personality. In other words, don't leave it so stark that it looks sterile. A great addition to an Elegant bedroom might be a fake fireplace with an ornate mantel. On that mantel, you might place a silver candelabra, an Oriental vase, a series of small gold-toned boxes. On your bedside tables, you might have groupings of family pictures all in the same style frame (the unornamented streamlined type in all gold or all silver), a collection of Steuben glass figures, or a single bud vase that you fill weekly.

Sporty/Country/Southwestern

I WOULD HAVE the most fun building this type of bedroom because it lends itself to the whimsical and creative. If you took my bedroom and transformed it to a Sporty look, you would buy floral or thickly striped linens and use a handmade quilt (or a copy) on the bed. You would add a wicker trunk at the foot of the bed and fill it with thick blankets. You'd either remove the shutters or leave them, using a stagecoach or balloon shade over them. You could even make café curtains with zigzag piping edges. (Another great and easy way to finish the hem of a curtain is to buy a string of fuzzy balls and sew them along the edge. Buy extra strings to use as tiebacks.)

If I wanted a Sporty bedroom, I might have some fun with the bed tables. I'd use a stack of antique leather luggage, a stack of floral hatboxes, or even wood packing crates. I would replace the wing chair with a ladderback or Mission-style chair, perhaps with a wood ottoman in front. I'd load the bookshelves with folk art, wood duck decoys, baskets, etc. I'd hide my TV and VCR in a tall pine armoire. I'd make a picture board—use a piece of plywood covered in fabric, then sew on horizontal rows of edging tape, and glue on pieces of molding around the edges—and load it with favorite photos. Last, I'd leave the wood floors, but cover them with rag or hooked area rugs.

Modern

A MODERN BEDROOM has a sleek, high-tech look to it. The trick is to keep it from looking empty, like no one lives there. After all, this isn't a museum, it's your home. And nowhere is warmth more needed than in your bedroom. If you started with my bedroom, here's what you'd need to change to make a Modern room spectacular, yet homey:

First, paint the walls—probably white. Think of the walls as a canvas (we'll hang things on them in just a moment). You could add a black-and-white geometric-shaped wallpaper border either at the top of the room, like mine, or at chair-rail height (use a black chair rail and apply border right above. Wow!) My Plantation shutters would be fine in this room because they're white, but if you want to stay strictly Modern, replace them with white or black mini-blinds. A straight valance above (maybe in your wallpaper pattern) will add a warmer feel. A wing chair would be at home in a Modern room if it were covered in black leather; or how about a black fabric with white polka-dots? You see how fabric changes everything?

Here's one simple idea to transform a not-quite-Modern bed (like mine) into a cozy personality statement: Buy strips of molding or small plaster discs (at home-improvement centers), paint them black or white, and glue them to the ceiling (with the strips, make a rectangle over the bed; with the discs, glue them over the corners of the bed). Buy a sheer black fabric, like chiffon, and hang it in two-foot-wide sections from the corners of the molding or from the discs (staple it). Let the sections drape over the corners of the bed, all the way to the floor. Boy, is this cozy.

The finishing touches in a Modern bedroom are linens and accessories. For linens, you could go with all one color or buy each piece in a different color (it's like layering a jacket over a vest over a shirt). Use a white bottom sheet, a black-and-white-striped top sheet, a black tailored dust ruffle, black and red and white pillows. For accessories, you might use black or chrome-plated picture frames, three floor-length mirrors hung in a row, chrome Hanson swing lamps, a grouping of black candles, a zebra-print throw or, better yet, rug.

Romantic

MY SUMMER-LOOK bedroom is almost Romantic. The hanging mosquito netting and soft white linens give it a sort of "Out of Africa" feel. You could also do the same trick (fabric hanging from ceiling) I described for a Modern room, but with white or floral fabric. My groupings of treasures that say "me" also add to the cozy, Romantic tone. To make it more so, I could add fussy, ruffly drapes with a matching dust ruffle, and fabric skirts to cover the bookcases. I would probably add a lace bedspread with an antique quilt folded at the foot of the bed.

If you are shopping for a new bed, consider brass or wrought iron for a Romantic bedroom. They have a lightness about them that adds the feminine quality you are looking for. Pile the bed with lots of pillows and maybe a few dolls or antique teddy bears. A white wicker secretary (this is a little tray that fits over your legs when you are sitting in bed) filled with stationery and books is as practical as it is stylish.

Accessories in this room would include lots and lots of candles, a piece of lace thrown over a lamp shade, a ceiling fan, and most definitely photos of loved ones in groupings.

As for the flooring, I might pickle the hardwood floors and use area rugs, or I might use a soft pastel color wall-to-wall carpet.

Eclectic

AS I'VE SAID, my bedroom is really Eclectic, even though I made it feel Classic. Chances are your bedroom will be Eclectic, too, if only because you need to keep the major pieces of furniture you already own. If you inherited a bedroom "suite" (this used to be the first type of furniture every set of newlyweds bought, so there are a lot of them around) but you don't really like it, there's plenty you can still do. Paint it, change the knobs on the dressers, cover the bed tables with pieces of fabric. You could even cover all of the pieces of the bed— the headboard, footboard, and side rails—with fabric (use quilt batting for padding and then staple fabric over it). In an instant, you'll have a whole new look and that is really what Eclectic is. It's a mix of styles, sure, but it is very up-to-date.

The first thing you should do if you aren't sure what type of room you want is to go shopping for linens. What you like will give you ideas for what else you might like in the room. I suggest shopping for linens first because, in my experience, if you paint or wallpaper first, it's nearly impossible to then find sheets in just the right shade of peach or green or blue. You may have a picture in your mind of the type of sheets you want, but I guarantee you, you'll never find them (then you'll use what you have and the look will be all wrong). Once you've bought sheets and a comforter (or blanket or bedspread), you'll see where you're going. Are the sheets in soft colors and patterns? Are they bold slashes of color? Are they crisp health-spa white?

Next you can choose paint or wallpaper, carpet, window treatments, and the big furniture for the room. One thing leads to another, and sooner or later you'll discover your Eclectic style.

Children's Rooms

SOME PEOPLE HAVE the philosophy that decorating kids' rooms doesn't matter. You just give them all the hand-me-downs and leftovers, because you think they don't care. I don't believe this. Each child has a different personality and their room should reflect who they are. They should feel comfortable in their own room. Also, no matter how neat your kid is, you're still going to have to go in there and help clean. Make it easier on yourself—and them—by providing a place for everything.

You start with the basics and build, just like any other room. So you have a bed, a dresser (I think bins in the closet are better because then the kids can see all their clothes at a glance, and it opens up floor space for them to play), a desk if they're school age (even if they're not, plan to add this later), and a place to put toys.

If you did pile all the hand-me-downs in their room, update them by sponge-painting the furniture, changing drawer knobs, using a fun area rug over the existing carpet, etc. If you are buying new furniture and accessories, give some thought to the future and buy things they can grow into. Consider bunk beds or trundle beds for when sleepovers happen every weekend. Don't cover the whole room in Winnie-the-Pooh wallpaper, because when your cute little boy turns six, he'll hate it. Don't force a lacy pink bedroom on a tomboy; chances are she won't change.

Try to find accessories to put on the walls that reflect their interests. Sports pennants, a shelf of dolls, prints of dinosaurs, pictures of their friends, a set of stick-on planets, etc. As for finding places to put all of their stuff, and they do have a lot of it, try these ideas: If your child goes to school or day care, he or she will bring home a daily barrage of "artwork." There are a few things you can do with it: You can leave it lying around where it will drive you nuts; send select samples to grandparents; create a gallery somewhere in your house to hang it;

throw it away (what parent hasn't made a midnight trip to the trash bin?); or you can buy a flat file (available in cardboard from Lillian Vernon, in wood at art stores) and store all of their little treasures in *their* room. You can even use this flat file as their bedside table.

As for toys and games, you can buy any number of bins and cases (try Rubbermaid's suitcase-style case, it's great) and put them on bookcases, or you can look at furniture made for just this purpose. The best source I've found is Whitney Bros. Company (800-225-5381). Call them and they will direct you to the nearest distributor. They make furniture for nursery schools, so each piece is made especially to store "stuff." Especially wonderful are their wall units that have eight separate cubbys in them. The wall units are roomy enough to stow all their books and games, and still have one or two cubbys left open to create child-size groupings.

Groupings in a child's room are just as important as they are in yours. The reason is that kids are natural collectors. They may start out collecting rocks (yes, I know a kid who does), but they will eventually move on to items that really tell you something about their personality. How wonderful to encourage their interests!

Frank and I helped decorate both our granddaughter's rooms. You'll see pictures of Hannah's room in the book, but we're not quite finished with Jenna's yet. (We had to do Hannah's in a hurry because she now has a new little sister.) Hannah's room is very feminine, yet not so little girly that she won't be just as happy with it ten years from now. She has a four-poster bed that I draped with really inexpensive fabric. I tied knots in the two ends and let them hang down (I didn't even finish the ends of the fabric). As she grows, we can change the fabric to reflect her new tastes. (In Jenna's room, I just bought sheets to match the Laura Ashley ones on the bed and hung them in the four corners of her ma-hogany four-poster.)

We deliberately chose grown-up fabrics in colors you wouldn't expect in a kid's room—sage, tans, off-white, lace—for Hannah's room because it's more lasting. She might like Elmo this year, but turn to Barbie tomorrow. This way she can bring in the things she likes whenever she wants . . . but the basic decor will stay the same.

We bought her chest of drawers at an unfinished furniture store and had an artist paint a country scene on it. (We bought the cheval mirror there, too, so she can see herself when she plays dress-up.) Both girls have little versions of grown-up furniture. Hannah has a ruffly armchair and ottoman, and Jenna has a wing chair and ottoman to go with her more traditional-style room.

The most creative thing we did in Hannah's room (and I really have to credit Frank here) is we bought two copies of a book of fables and tore all of the pages out of the books. We framed the prints and had the framer place the accompanying text pages on the back of each frame. Hannah can take them down and have her parents read them to her and then turn them over to see the pictures. She loves them and it was cheap, cheap, cheap! You can see that by treating your child's room like a special place, it will make your child feel like you want her to . . . special.

Chapter 14

Your Kitchen

Hmmm . . . kitchens. My best friends and my worst enemies. You know how much I love to cook and eat (it's the eating part that gets me in trouble), so you must know how important I feel a kitchen is to any home. It is the heart of your home. Whether you plan it that way or not, it's where everyone will gather. Most of the important conversations I had with my parents growing up took place in the kitchen . . . maybe because it was neutral territory. Most houses are designed so that the kitchen is in the middle of it all. So, even if you hate to cook, you'll still probably spend more time in your kitchen than in any other room in the house.

Of course, if you love to cook, you'll want your kitchen to be a focal point. While the design is important—and it must go with the rest of your home— you have to think about function as well. You have to have a place to store your pots and pans, your blender, your coffee machine. You'll want to keep cookbooks within easy reach. You may want a wine rack with glasses close by. All of these things add to the comfort level of the cook. So when you are planning the "look" of your kitchen, give some thought to how you will use it as well.

You can get great ideas for kitchens from magazines and visiting kitchen design showrooms. Even the superstores offer fully set-up samples of real kitchens (along with trained consultants to answer your questions). Use these resources to gather information on what's available before you change a thing. You'd hate it if you spent a fortune, and then discovered the perfect under-the-counter recycling bins that would have fit great had you only moved the stove over three inches. Do a bit of poking around first, whether you are planning a complete overhaul or just a design personality change.

My Kitchen

MY KITCHEN IN New York is small, as are most of them in this city. It's what's referred to as a galley kitchen. Short and narrow. Sure, I would have loved an eat-in kitchen, but I would have had to sacrifice a part of my dining room to do it, and I wasn't willing to do that. What I did instead was to make this tiny kitchen as charming and warm as I could. It's inviting and functions beautifully. Even though the appliances and cabinets are new, I was able to maintain the Classic look that I have in the rest of the apartment by using the colors and textures that tie it into the dining room, which is right next door.

I used a striped washable wallpaper that matches the green of the dining-room walls. The green faux-marble tile—it's press-and-peel, so easy to install—has an old-world look to it and the rich, dark wood of the cabinets is the same as my dining-room table. The tiny, framed pictures—botanical prints are at home in any Classic room—you see on the wall are postcards that I bought while on a trip. I keep my flour and sugar in chrome jars that are actually from a medical-supply store. (Doctors use them to store tongue depressors and cotton balls.) This is a great example of wanting a certain look, but not wanting to spend too much money. These jars have the look of silver—which would look nice, but get beat up in a kitchen—yet cost so little.

I had the luxury—in this apartment—of building a brand-new kitchen, but you may have to work with what you have, either because of the expense or because you are renting and are not allowed to make major changes. There are two things you should know before you embark on a kitchen transformation: One, redoing a kitchen is the number-one factor in the resale of your home. You will get back every penny you put into it (maybe more). So, if you are thinking about where to spend the money that you have, know that a new kitchen is the best investment. And second, there are inexpensive changes you can make that will, really, give you a whole new look. Some changes are permanent (and therefore require a landlord's approval), but some can be made using design techniques alone. Here are some simple ideas to make your kitchen a room you love to be in.

From an All-White Kitchen to . . .

IF YOU MOVE into a house or apartment and the kitchen has all white cabinets, white floors, white countertops, white appliances, etc., think of it as a blank palette. If it's a standard white kitchen, the sink is probably stainless steel. This is a Modern, stark look (great beginnings if that's your personality) but still needs a jolt of style. If you are going for a Sporty/Country, Romantic, Elegant, or Eclectic look, you'll have to change more, but it can be done so easily. Follow me . . .

Classic

THIS IS MY kitchen. If you want a Classic kitchen in your home, but have the all-white thing going, here's what to do. If I hadn't started from scratch, I would probably have taken the white cabinets and painted them a deep red (to give the feel of wood) and lacquered them for a richer look. My wallpaper is a small stripe that might be found in a much older house (that way, when you look at my kitchen, you can't really tell when it was built—could be last week, could be last century). But to really bring in a very Classic feel, Frank and I also added the heavy wood molding you see at the top of the wall and cabinets. This is so inexpensive! I wish I had before and after photos of this part of the kitchen to show you how dramatic the change was. So simple, yet so perfect.

Our floor is made from stick-on tiles, as I've said before, so you can buy these and put them down right over what is already there. While my tiles are green, you could also choose a lighter color, but it should have some pattern to it, like marble or granite.

A Classic kitchen is really from another time, so try to consider that when you choose all of your elements. For instance, wallpaper is more appropriate than tile. If you don't want to hang wallpaper behind your stove, consider a single sheet of copper. It's very period appropriate and looks terrific. For this kind of kitchen, I would choose to bring in a wood table rather than build an island unit to eat on. If you have the room, create a cozy corner, using this table, and keep your tablecloths and tableware in fabrics and styles that suit a Classic look. Finally, about lighting: Because electric lighting wasn't available during the time you're trying to replicate, choose recessed ceiling lights and under-cabinet light bars to keep fixtures hidden from view.

Elegant

PULLING OFF AN Elegant kitchen when you're starting with all white (especially if the cabinets are a squarish, flat-front variety) is tough, but you'll be surprised at how a little ingenuity can get the job done. An Elegant kitchen calls for wood raised-panel cabinets, a granite countertop, marble floors . . . Whew! Who can afford that? You can, if you follow my advice. The first thing you'll have to do is either paint your cabinets a deep, rich color (you can stick with white painted wood if the cabinets are the rounded raised-panel variety, just coat them with a high-gloss white paint), or, and this is the best, trot on down to Home Depot or Ikea and just buy new raised-panel doors and laminate strips to fill in the gaps. Buying the doors alone will save you, and I'm not kidding, thousands of dollars. Change the drawer pulls and handles to simple round brass ones.

Next, for a countertop, look at Formica (there are other brand names, but this is usually sold everywhere) chips and find a design that simulates granite. You would not believe the quality of this stuff. I think it looks like the real thing. For an Elegant kitchen, you might choose a deep green, a white with black flecks, a pale, pale pink . . . take a look. A contractor can apply this laminate right over your existing countertop (a four-by-eight sheet costs about $80, and maybe $200 to install, compared with $1,000 for the same size granite or marble).

Your next stop will be the flooring department. You will find marble-looking press-and-peel tiles and sheets of linoleum from every manufacturer. The styles are endless. Go for a rich green, a white/gray, a pale salmon. Measure your floor area and take the tiles home to install yourself. This is easy.

Okay, you've transformed the big stuff, and you saved money didn't you? Now start to add the little bits that really bring out your Elegant personality. A crystal ice bucket to hold utensils. A small Oriental rug in front of the sink. A small ornate mirror framed by two tiny wall sconces. A countertop wine rack to hold the wine you'll celebrate with when you're done.

Sporty/Country/Southwestern

FOR THIS TYPE of kitchen, you will want to bring in your Country colors—blues, oranges, browns . . . but don't forget the white! You can't ignore the white cabinets and countertops. Because you're keeping what you have, you have to blend the white into the room but make it a less overwhelming presence. To make everything work together, you might choose a blue-and-white-striped wallpaper; change the stainless steel sink to a blue enamel one; make blue, pale orange, and white plaid café curtains; and change the drawer pulls from white to a deep orange. On the walls you might hang a bunch of dried flowers in your colors or even hang a row of copper pots (to accent the orange tones) on wood pegs along one wall.

One way to change white cabinets into something else without just painting them (although you could—sponge-painted cabinets in a Country kitchen are charming) is to add strips of molding to the door faces. Buy molding at any lumberyard (they may even cut it to size for you) and paint it in one of your colors before applying it to doors. You can then glue—use a strong epoxy—the strips to the face of your doors (no nails needed) in a rectangle to create a raised panel effect. I did this in the first kitchen I redesigned, and I can tell you, it looked fantastic.

If you want to add just a bit more color to break the eye from your white countertop to the cabinets above, you can apply square tile to the area in between (it's called a backsplash). A great look for a country kitchen is to choose tiles in white and two different colors and arrange them randomly. You should buy these tiles at a home-improvement center (for about twenty-nine cents each) rather than at a tile store, because these stores will allow you to buy just a few instead of a whole box. These tiles are fairly thin and can be cut easily, allowing you to do the job yourself. Another great Country tile look is to use all white square tiles and then apply grout in one of your colors in between them.

You can keep your white countertop if you added color and softened lines elsewhere, but if you choose to keep the white cabinets instead, you may want to try a butcher-block countertop. It looks very Sporty/Country and you can use it as a big cutting board.

Finally, finish off your Country look with accessories: a wicker ceiling fan with light fixture, mason jars filled with colored pasta, a checked mat in front of the sink, and some fun things like a cactus cookie jar.

Modern

IF YOU HAD to choose a palette to start from to build a Modern kitchen, this is it. Your canvas is ready for some finishing touches. To make your high-tech look stand out, you may stay with your white cabinets or you may paint them (a glossier white or another color in your scheme), or you could face them with stainless-steel panels (you can buy sheets of punched metal ones from a lumberyard—they're used to make radiator enclosures). Certainly change the drawer pulls and handles to a shiny black or red or steel.

Tile the backsplash and the area over the stove in all-black or all-red or all-blue shiny tiles. Use a same-color grout or use white grout for a geometric look. For the flooring, one choice is a black faux-marble linoleum, another is a sheet of industrial rubber (you'll see it in restaurant kitchens). You might also just leave the white floor and put down monochromatic area rugs in one of your colors. Cover windows with blinds in black, red, blue, or for a super high-tech look, choose stainless steel or copper.

A great light fixture for a Modern kitchen is a pendant lamp (or a row of them) that has a flat downward-facing shade. They can be installed on a cord that retracts to provide different levels of light. I have seen them in every color and in metal finishes, like copper and steel.

Because this is a stark look, try to bring warmth to a Modern kitchen. One way is to think of things not normally seen in a kitchen and come up with new uses for them. Some ideas are wire clothing bins to hold linens and potholders, black lacquer boxes filled with fruit, a CD holder to stack the dessert plates you collect. The point is to show a little of your personality to soften this very linear room.

Romantic

YOU ARE STARTING off ahead of the game here because white is a big part of the Romantic look. Still, the harsh line of all-white everything needs to be broken up for a truly Romantic room. Let's start with the cabinets. Try sponge-painting in pastels, or use other decorative painting techniques like stenciling or washing. The point is to soften the look of all that white. For upper cabinets, you may try cutting out the center sections of the doors and replacing them with chicken wire or a lace fabric panel. If you really love wood cabinets, buy new doors in a light maple or white oak. Replace drawer pulls and handles with some from your color scheme.

Choose a floral washable wallpaper in a tiny print (if you kept the white cabinets, make sure there is some white in the paper), or paint the walls in a soft color. For flooring, you could apply a pinkish marble linoleum tile. If you have wood floors in the kitchen already (aren't you lucky), sand them down to the raw wood and pickle or paint them. Make curtains that suit your Romantic look; try a floral valance (perhaps in the same print as the wallpaper) with sheer panels hanging beneath or white shutters with a lace swag on top.

You chose this look because you like having the things you love around you, so bring some of them into the kitchen. Cover a wood shelf with antique lace and place on it a fabric-covered box to hold your recipes; wrap a cylinder in satin ribbon to hold your utensils; hang small prints from silver bow hooks.

Eclectic

FOR AN ECLECTIC kitchen you are going to borrow ideas from all of the other styles we've talked about here. There are so many different ways you can do it that I can't possibly think of them all, so I am going to tell you once again to stay with your three basic colors and to keep things simple. These are the rules for every style, but more so for Eclectic because you can so quickly fall into having no style at all. Before you know it, you have white cabinets, black canisters, yellow walls . . . go slowly and do an inventory every now and then to check yourself.

Chapter 15

Your Bathrooms

I f you want to update and restyle your home, the bathrooms can be the best places to start. They're small, making the job more manageable and easier to redo if you don't quite get it right the first time. Renovating a bathroom is a job that can cost $5,000 or as little as $50, depending on the extent of the renovation. Before you begin to think about what you want, take inventory of what you have. Are the fixtures—sink, toilet, tub, faucets—in good shape? Are they the style and color you want? Are they cracked or stained in places that matter? Is the sink black, the toilet white, and the tub tan? If you have any of these problems, I would buy new. With careful shopping you can replace each of these items for under $100 each ($200 for a tub).

If you do replace these items, remember that they are basics, which means that new ones will have to be in one of your three colors and the style should be as simple as possible (to allow for later redesigns. Who knows—next year, you may want a Romantic master bath?). The tricks you'll learn about vanities, wallpaper, paint, and mirrors, will be enough to transform simple fixtures into the style you are aiming for.

My Bathroom

AS IS THE REST of my New York apartment, the master bathroom has a Classic feel to it. It looks old-world and expensive, but truly, we didn't spend very much. We bought plain wainscotting strips from Home Depot, fit them together, and stained and finished them to a deep, warm color. The countertop is actually a piece of wood that Frank and I painted in a faux marble and then finished with a waterproof glaze.

It's all about tricking the eye. You may not be able to afford an Armani jacket, but if you find a good enough copy, no one will know the difference. Decorating is the same way. I could have bought a $300 sink at a designer showroom, but I found the one I wanted at a home-improvement store; I think it was $50.

You have to figure out where to put your money and where it matters. The only thing for which I spent more than I wanted was the faucet. If you look at the pictures of my bathroom, you'll see that the faucet and hot and cold water taps are three separate pieces. I really felt that I needed that look for my Classic room, but it's more expensive (one-piece faucets cost a lot less). It was the accessory I chose to really bring out the antique personality I wanted in the room. Decorating is all about making choices.

Classic

YOU'VE JUST READ a little bit about my Classic bathroom and how I pulled it together from scratch. You don't need to strip your bathroom to the bare studs like I did to have the same effect; there are minor changes you can make to achieve the Classic look. Here's an easy one: Change your white toilet seat to a wood one. Instant ancient!

From the floor up, here's what to do. The choices for a Classic floor are wood, small tiles (I have six-sided ones in mine), terra-cotta, or—for a Classic Italian look—mosaic tiles. If you have thick ceramic tile down now, you'll have to pull it up, but if you have thin linoleum or plastic tile, you can apply your new choice right over it. Simply screw down a piece of quarter-inch plywood over the floor to provide a stable base for the new flooring. Another easy and cheap option would be to lay down a sisal rug over the floor you hate. This is great in a powder room, but can work in a bath if you take care to use a bath mat over it.

The sink area can contain a standard vanity cabinet or you can use a table with a hole cut in it, or you can even have a freestanding sink with no cabinet. A Classic sink should be round or oval and in a white or off-white. For authenticity, faucets should be brass (or brushed brass) and each component should be a separate piece. If you can't afford that, look for one-piece faucets in curvy, antique styles.

On your walls you may choose wainscotting, like I did, or wallpaper or decorative painting. You will want to choose a small print for this small room, and it has to be washable. For the tub and shower area, choose a tile that matches one of your three colors. If there is maroon and tan and green in your wallpaper, any one of those colors would work for your tile.

Choose your linens and curtains to complement your Classic style. If you have wallpaper, make curtains and a shower curtain from the matching fabric. Use towels and washcloths in one or more of your three colors. Even if your bathroom transformation is not absolutely authentic, these accessories will pull the room together.

Last, bring some of your own personality into the bathroom. Sure, it has to be functional, but it can be pretty, too. Place a grouping of antique silver shaving accessories on a shelf above the sink; frame those black-and-white prints of your great-grandparents and hang them over the toilet; or put a basket of dried flowers in the corner of the tub.

Elegant

THIS SORT OF bathroom can be enormous and opulent, filled with a massive whirlpool tub, a bidet, and a heated towel rack. Or, it can have the usual sink, tub, and toilet and just *look* elegant and opulent. It's the clean lines and shiny surfaces that will give it that rich look, not the thousands you could spend on fixtures.

There are two ways to go to achieve an Elegant bath: all-white (but softer than a Modern look) fixtures, vanity, and wall tiles with marble-looking floors, or off-white fixtures with cabinets made from a dark wood, like cherry or walnut, and pale floors and wall tiles. In either case, the knobs and faucets should be brass (to give the look of gold) or chrome (for a silver look).

You'll bring other colors into the room through the wallpaper (choose a quiet pattern, like thin stripes or small polka-dots) or paint and other accessories. If you use wallpaper, buy matching fabric for curtains and a shower curtain. You could even use this fabric to make a tailored skirt for under the sink, instead of a vanity.

Elegant accessories might include brass or silver-plated cups and soap dishes, a brass or silver swing-arm mirror, or a crystal bowl filled with decorative soaps.

Sporty/Country/Southwestern

IF YOU NEED to work with what you have, this kind of bath will probably be the easiest to transform. Two changes are all you need to make a Sporty statement—it doesn't matter what color your fixtures are; they could even be black. First, replace your vanity cabinet. You could buy an oak cabinet (about $100 at home-improvement centers) or you could paint the one that is there. You could paint it a solid color, or you could use a decorative-painting technique. Washing and sponge-painting look great in this kind of bath (you could even do the walls in the same technique). Another option is to remove the vanity entirely and make a fabric skirt for around the sink.

The second change you need to make is to remove the medicine cabinet. If it has lights attached—we'll have to think about other lighting options, but that's easy—hang a bar of round light bulbs (they come in anywhere from two to six bulbs) over the new mirror you are going to buy. Now, either buy an oak mirror or buy a plain one and paint it in the same technique you used for the vanity. Trust me, even if you have avocado-green tiles, replacing these two items will make your bathroom feel up-to-date and Sporty.

Of course, you have to continue and add some fun accessories like wood pegs to hold towels, maybe a high wicker shelf with a plant (real or fake) in a terra-cotta pot, a basket of rolled up hand towels, a grouping of desert landscapes, etc.

Modern

A MODERN BATHROOM, like the rest of a Modern house, is stark and linear. That means a very monochromatic look—black-and-white, red-and-white, white-and-chrome—with sculptural accessories. If you start with all-white fixtures, you may need to do as little as changing the faucets and knobs to a high-polished chrome (you'll need to wipe them down after each use to keep the shine), changing the white toilet seat to black, installing silver blinds, and maybe using a chrome coat rack to hold your black-and-white towels. These small changes will say Modern before you can.

If your fixtures are, say, pastel blue, you can either change them or use that blue as one of your three colors, but play it down. You might retile the bath stall in white tile, but at the top make a border of alternating two-by-two-inch square tiles in your pastel blue, white, and navy (to introduce your third color). Paint the walls in a bright white and hang Art Deco prints in pastel blue and navy square-edged frames. Bring in accessories like navy-blue shutters, towel racks, and sink accessories. To tie all of the colors together, use white one-foot square tiles on the floor—with pastel blue grout—and a navy-blue fluffy are a rug.

Romantic

YOU CHOSE THIS style because you are all bubble baths and candles, so, of course, the bathroom is going to be your favorite room to decorate. What you are really making is a place where you can hide and relax, so think along those lines when you are planning this room. Where will you sit to cut your nails? (A tiny tufted ottoman that can double as a step stool for your kids.) Where will you stash your candles, matches to light them, and a romantic novel for your bath? (Either on a shelf in the tub or in a wicker box placed on the countertop.) Where will you hang your thick, pale-yellow bath towels that you spent a little more for because they felt so good? (On a row of antique cut-glass doorknobs you picked up at a garage sale for pennies.) Geez . . . just writing about this room makes me want to run right over and take a bubble bath!

One of the things you will want in a Romantic bath is a source of soft light. In my Connecticut house, Frank ran an electrical wire up through the vanity and countertop; we can now have tiny lamps next to the sink, for those moments when a harsh overhead light is, well, too harsh.

For curtains and drapes, you will want to choose floral fabrics in soft pastels. You can use this fabric alone on the windows and tub enclosure, or you can mix it with lace panels. On the windows, you may even want to try shutters with a swag over them, mixing the fabric and lace together.

Eclectic

IF YOUR HOME is Eclectic, your bathroom should be, too. You've already established that you like a little of this and a little of that, so here's your chance to put all of your ideas into action. As I said in the beginning of this chapter, because bathrooms are small, they are great rooms to experiment in. Many bathrooms have to be Eclectic because we are working with what we have. I know a lot of homes built in the fifties or sixties have a sort of Art Deco look: pink tiles with a black border and pink tub, toilet, and sink. How would you update this? First, you'd buy a rosy floral shower curtain and then sew a border along the sides and bottom in, maybe, a black-and-white stripe with pink piping. You might also make a valance out of the same striped fabric and hang it above the shower curtain on a tension rod. Just this little addition will totally change the look of your bathroom from tired to fashionable.

Remember to tie your bathroom into your bedroom somehow; this is especially important in an Eclectic bath. In my New York apartment, I use towels similar to my linens—animal prints, reds, and tans. You might choose a reverse version of your wallpaper to tie your rooms together: Thick white stripes with thin yellow ones in the bath, and thick yellow stripes with thin white ones in the bedroom. Other ways to make the rooms mesh are to keep the woods similar (oak bed, oak vanity) or to keep two of your three bedroom colors for the bath (if your bedroom is salmon, pale yellow, and green, your bath might be salmon, pale yellow, and white).

In an Eclectic bathroom, you might also try these ideas: Hang a glass shelf around the room, about a foot below the ceiling, and fill it with groupings of things you love. Add a few picture lights . . . and wow . . . you've created art! Or how about this: Start with a white painted wall and then glue black-and-white photos of your family to it, apply a coat of waterproof varnish to preserve it, and you've got a gallery of memories.

Bathroom Lighting

DON'T BE AFRAID to tear out what is there and change it (if you're renting, save the fixtures and replace them when you move). Think beyond a medicine chest with two bars of fluorescent running up the sides (no one looks good in those lights). All of the lighting choices I talk about in Chapter Ten and the Glossary will work in a bathroom. Check them out and give yourself room to experiment.

Mirrors

YOU CAN HAVE a lot of fun with mirrors in a bathroom. You can hang one large mirror or a grouping of smaller ones. You can paint the frame to match any decor; this is the perfect room to hang that unusual mirror you bought at an auction and don't know what to do with. One of my favorite looks in a bathroom is an entire wall of mirrored glass. Fortunately, this is also one of the least expensive mirror options. You can buy a plain piece of mirror (make sure it's at least ⅜ of an inch thick) about four-feet by four-feet for about $75 installed (call a glass store). The beauty of it is that it goes with any style and doubles the size of the room.

Chapter 16

Art & Stuff

You've pulled together the basics of your rooms—the sofas, the rugs, the tables—and now you are ready to add the finishing touches. This is where you show off your personal style. This is the fun part. Really fun, because you are limited only by the scope of your imagination. This is the part we all love . . . shopping, looking, searching. Going to funky little stores. Antique stores. Flea markets. Anywhere and everywhere. Finding goodies. Some art— some real, some personal. Stuff that says you. This is accessorizing. And if you don't like the mix, you can always put things away and reintroduce them later.

What falls into this category of accessories? Things like paintings, prints, sculpture, mirrors, pillows, throws, small interesting tables, place mats, candlesticks, shelves, plants . . . you see, it's all the stuff that's fun to buy and arrange. Here's when you are allowed to see something and buy it just because you like it. Of course, you have to have a place to put it where it works, but by this point you're such a pro that that should be no problem.

You may like to have a theme for each room, like sailing, for instance (that's what I did for my apartment in New York), and then, of course, you choose your accessories accordingly. Or, you may like a particular period (in my Connecticut house everything is from the seventeenth and eighteenth centuries) and choose accessories of all types that fit that style. You may be more eclectic and choose items from all over the place. That's fine as long as the accessories are artfully arranged and don't overpower the room. You may even find when shopping for accessories that you want to completely redo the room because you find something you absolutely love, and you want to make a go of it no matter what. Hey, you like what you like, and you have to go with that when choosing the extras for your rooms.

Your home will tell people things about you instantly, and you will feel a certain way when you are in your home. What people see should be style first and then little hints about your personality. What *you* should feel is comfortable first and then little "aahs" of delight when you spy your finishing touches. That print you picked up on your honeymoon (I always buy art when on vacation rather than silly souvenirs; I spend a little more, but get a wonderful remem-

brance of my trip), the Navajo rug you lugged home from New Mexico, those funny-shaped bottles you haggled over at a flea market. These are all of the things that make your home yours—not mine, not anyone else's.

Classic

ON YOUR COFFEE OR END TABLES: You may not have a coffee table, but an antique trunk or three wood crates grouped together. On this surface, you might place an antique plate, a bowl of richly colored marbles, a needlepoint box, a stack of leatherbound books, candles of varying sizes, a silver cigar box, a child's china tea set.

Waves of Pleasure

A friend of mine who is an artist always has a blue tablecloth on her dining-room table, but with a twist. She lays it with the corners hanging over each side (baring the actual corners of the table) and then bunches it up a little to create waves. There's also a collection of beautiful shells in the middle. For a while I just didn't get it. Every time I walked by that table I had to straighten out that tablecloth. She'd bunch it up; I'd straighten it out. It finally dawned on me that she created this special effect on purpose; tablecloth waves with shells. It was her way of making a little ocean in her dining room. Once I figured it out, I got a kick of delight when I saw it. ❖

ON YOUR WALLS: Hang an old (or new) tapestry, a large piece of fabric, loose or stretched onto a wood frame, aged postcards, or odd-shaped ornate mirrors. Botanical prints fit a Classic room. You can find great prints in any bookstore. Tear them out and frame them. An antique Christening dress, hung on a wood hanger or a silver-spoon collection are interesting accents.

AROUND YOUR HOUSE: A corner filled with antique candle molds, milk jugs, and butter churns. A shelf full of china sugar bowls and creamers. A half-finished painting and a collection of paintbrushes on your bathroom counter. Tin food containers on your kitchen counter with a vase of antique utensils next to it.

If you like old things, as I do, but are on a limited budget, these little collections of things are where you should spend your money. You can pick up one or two every now and then for very little money and slowly build a fine collection.

Elegant

ON YOUR COFFEE OR END TABLES: This style of home does not have a lot of things lying around and those that are are there for a reason. Your groupings have to be simple, yet stunning. Use lots of crystal, real silver, real china. That doesn't mean boring. If you have interests, perhaps the English countryside, you might choose to put a pile of books by celebrated English authors on your table, along with a pile of antique quill pens.

ON YOUR WALLS: Elegant art is subdued, not flashy. You can choose inexpensive prints that look like real oils. Unless you are having the curator of the Met over for dinner, probably no one will notice they are fakes. You will want brass or crystal wall sconces, perhaps framing an etched-glass ornately framed mirror. Nothing is more dramatic in an Elegant room than a tapestry hung on the wall. Again, it doesn't have to be an antique. You can find plenty of fabrics with scenes on them and have the ends bound. You might even add a fringe and tassel along the bottom.

You might also search for antique-looking maps for your walls. I have seen them in books. You can tear out the pages and frame them. They give a real old-world feel to an Elegant room.

AROUND YOUR HOUSE: The lines of an Elegant home are simple, so take care not to add clutter instead of style. A simple crystal vase with a single orchid says more about this style than two dozen roses do. You might try a collection of big, long candles (I mean long, like four feet tall) set on the floor to add interest to a boring corner and, by all means, leave out your grandmother's silver tea set on the dining-room sideboard.

Sporty/Country/Southwestern

ON YOUR COFFEE OR END TABLES: A bowl of fruit—real, dried, or made of stone or papier mâché. A piece of folk art (a wooden cowboy, brightly painted wood flowers, etc.). A pile of books on Native Americans. A wood or wicker box filled with coasters or napkins. Antique gardening tools. A coil of rope. Shells. Stacked baskets. Shaker boxes. A découpaged box tied with a raffia ribbon.

ON YOUR WALLS: An American flag. Old (or new) quilts. A collection of hats. A Navajo blanket. Sports' team pennants. Wood framed mirrors. Painted-frame mirror. Prints of desert flowers. Prints of birds. Photographs of land-scapes. Earthy-colored plates.

A R O U N D   Y O U R   H O U S E : Salt-and-pepper shaker collection on a shelf. Small plants on individual small shelves. A collection of wood walking sticks in a corner. Copper pots. Weathervanes. A carousel horse. Mason jars filled with colored pasta on your kitchen counter. A wrought-iron pot rack over the stove. You might gather a collection of framed photos and lean them on a chair rail in the dining room. Or for larger pieces of art, just lean them against a wall on the floor.

Find an idea that speaks to you and go all the way with it. For example: Make a grouping of a wood sailboat (buy new and stain sails with coffee to look old), shells, a tin sand pail holding a tiny rosemary bush, and a ship's clock and set on top of a lobster trap. Behind this grouping, you might have canvas drapes tied back with ropes to look like a ship's rigging.

Modern

O N   Y O U R   C O F F E E   T A B L E   A N D   E N D   T A B L E S : You may have a coffee table or you may use a stainless-steel box on wheels (road crews use these to pack speakers in), or a thick piece of glass held up by three black bowling balls. A Modern room gives you license to try all sorts of unusual items in every room. On top of your makeshift tables you might have a single red metal sculpture. You might have a steel bowl filled with glossy black marble balls. Try three tall, square, black or silver candles. A grouping of glossy lacquer boxes. Lucite picture frames.

O N   Y O U R   W A L L S : Big pieces of abstract art (you can even paint these yourself). A collection of rhinestone pins matted on black velvet. Tall, thin mirrors, either unframed or wide white painted frames. A grouping of Art Deco prints. A series of monochromatic plates in odd sizes. Steel mixing bowls on a kitchen wall.

A R O U N D   Y O U R   H O U S E : A Modern style allows you plenty of freedom to mix old with new. Don't shy away from antiques because you think a Modern house shouldn't have them. Try an antique rocking horse in the corner of the living room. Pierced-tin wall sconces in the hallways. A bright green canoe leaning against a wall.

Try to find everyday items that go with your house's personality, like black or stainless-steel canisters to hold flour and sugar on a kitchen counter, an architectural toilet-paper holder and towel rack, drawer pulls made from pieces of marble that are not uniform. It is these little things that will really bring out the personality. Also in the kitchen, you might replace the glass in cabinets with sheets of wire mesh for a more industrial look.

Romantic

ON YOUR COFFEE OR END TABLES: Instead of a traditional coffee/end table you might have white wicker picnic baskets or trunks. You might add a piece of floral fabric or lace. On top of that, you may have a collection of maybe fifteen photos of loved ones in curvy, unique frames. A Romantic room is all about feelings and displaying things that are close to your heart. Why not fill a padded pink box with treasures like love letters, sachets, porcelain hearts, and other items that make you feel lovely?

ON YOUR WALLS: Again, find items that evoke a certain time or place and customize them to fit your Romantic room. Hang pictures from ribbons topped off with a bow. Use mirrors with a real seashell border, a hand-painted frame, or a fabric-covered frame. Gather a collection of postcards and have them matted together in a color that matches your scheme. Hang scarves from individual wooden pegs.

AROUND YOUR HOUSE: Use lace on your kitchen shelves, instead of lining paper, and let the ends hang over the edge. Hang a floral or lacy curtain on a rod under your kitchen sink to soften the effect of all wood cabinets. Set up a folding screen in the bedroom and drape it with antique nightshirts. Install molding on the ceiling over your bed and attach a sheer floaty fabric to close around the bed.

Collecting or Just Collecting Dust

All of us have little collections of things. Hats. Porcelain figurines. Crystal animals. Snow globes. You know, stuff. But stuff you really like and would like to see every day. You can leave them lying around in no particular place (collecting dust) or make them into art. I have a friend who has over thirty antique demitasse spoons from all over the world. She found an antique glass-covered pipe rack in which the spoons hang beautifully. Now they are on display and, best of all, she never has to polish them! ❖

A Romantic house needs lots of candles in all sizes and shapes (don't forget to light them from time to time).

Eclectic

ON YOUR COFFEE OR END TABLES: This kind of room can have traditional wood tables, glass-topped ones, wrought-iron; you name it, you can have it if it goes with your colors and size of your room. On these tables you can steal ideas from all of the other rooms above, mix them, change them—that's what Eclectic is.

ON YOUR WALLS: If your room leans a little toward Classic, choose artwork that fits that style *and* your personality. Try hanging botanical prints, but in brighter frames. Use antique quilts, but maybe add a red-painted strip of wood at the top or bottom. If your rooms lean more toward Modern, try a mirror framed in stainless steel but more ornately decorated than one you would use in a strictly Modern room.

AROUND YOUR HOUSE: The key to this kind of home working well is to keep control of the clutter. Because you think you have no specific style, you may lapse into not trying. Don't let that happen. Keep things in their place and continue to arrange accessories that say something good about you.

Hanging Up

I like to hang things on walls. For one, it gets them out of the bottom of my closet, and two, they provide a little free art. The thing I hang is hats. I have a whole wall full of them. Since I almost always wear a hat, it also makes it easier to see what I have and what will match my outfit that day. You can hang whatever you want: scarves, dishes on wire holders, baskets, your kid's artwork, etc. Try it . . . if you don't like it, you can always take it down. ❖

Antiques and Collecting

I HAVE FILLED both of my homes with antiques and collections of things I've gathered over the years. These are not necessarily expensive things—although some are—but things I have picked up one at a time and added to my groupings. You can't just decide you are going to collect antique blue-patterned plates and run out and buy twenty today. That defeats the purpose of collecting, which is the searching and shopping and building. You'll remember where you bought each plate and connect it with some wonderful event or time. As your collection grows, your friends will notice it and, you'll see, you'll start to receive treasured pieces as gifts, making that piece even more valuable.

If you are collecting something that is an antique—anything over one hundred years old—you should really bone up on it. Go to the library or bookstore and read through guides that describe and price your treasures. Ask store owners detailed questions about where a piece came from and when it was made. Don't assume that just because something is in an antique store, that it really is an antique. Plenty of stores that claim to be antique stores mix newer merchandise with the old.

If you aren't collecting anything now, think about what things make you smile when you see them. When you go into a store, what do you instantly head for? When you're in someone else's home, what do you admire? Find something that really intrigues you and you'll find a hobby that will last for the rest of your life. Here are some ideas to think about:

❖ Antique tools. Make a grouping of smaller tools on a table, perhaps with a plant. Use larger tools, like a rake or a hay fork, either on the walls or leaning in a corner.

❖ China. Either something in a particular pattern, like Meissen (also called Blue Onion), or dishes of all types with similar things on them, like horses or ships.

❖ Old bottles. Use them together in a grouping as they are, or maybe fill them with different spiced vinegars and set on kitchen shelf.

❖ Stamps or wine labels. Both can be either mounted in frames or découpaged onto a wooden box.

❖ Thimbles, salt-and-pepper shakers, old keys, porcelain figurines. All can be grouped on a table or mounted in a glass display case. You can also buy tables with cases built in to the top and covered with glass.

❖ Glassware of different colors. All blue, all red, all clear with a purple tint from age. You can use groupings of glassware in any room, either on a table or on a shelf.

❖ Prints with a similar theme. Cows, jungle animals, flowers, maps, etc.

❖ Small wood boxes (even cigar boxes). Tie them in ribbons, cover them in fabric or wallpaper, stack them, use them to hold a grouping of candles.

❖ Baskets, new or antique. Group them in a corner or on a table, hang them on walls on single wooden pegs, fill them with fruits and vegetables.

❖ Antique easels, large or tabletop size. Use them all together or one in each room to display favorite artwork.

Glossary

Furniture Styles

IF YOU KNOW THE BASIC elements to look for when shopping for furniture styles, you will have a better sense of what you are buying. Many times, you will see combinations of these styles as designers try to combine the best of each to create yet another new look. This guide gives you the flavor of each style, and also helps you understand what the salespeople are talking about when they use the real terms for each piece. Of course, I can't list absolutely every style of furniture ever made, but I've covered most of the ones you'll need. You don't have to memorize this section, just know it's here for quick reference when you need it.

Chairs

Barcelona (1929)

Designed by Ludwig Mies van der Rohe, often considered the masterpiece of twentieth-century elegance. It is an armless leather chair with an X-shaped chrome base. Steel and leather, cantilevered seat. Very Modern.

Bentwood (1840)

Named for the technique of wetting wood and bending it into curved shapes, this is a round-backed chair, with the back and the seat made from woven rattan. Also made in rocking-chair styles.

Breuer Wassily (1925) and Cesca (1929)

Both of these chairs, designed by architect Marcel Breuer, are made from tubular steel. The Wassily has a back and seat of leather; the Cesca rattan. They are very Modern, coming out of the famed Bauhaus school in Germany.

Chippendale (1718–1779)

The most notable feature of Chippendale's chairs are the ornately carved, curved legs, ending in a claw-and-ball foot. Chair seats are upholstered, but the backs are usually carved in intricate patterns (although they can also be upholstered).

Empire (1801)

This style has a solid curved wood and upholstered back, although its most distinctive feature is the brass and gilt ornate appliqués. The Biedermeier style is based on Empire forms.

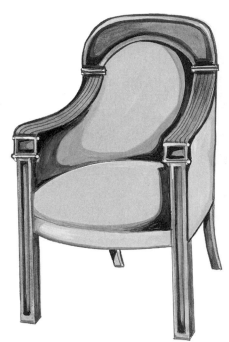

French Provincial (1600–1800)

This chair is a less formal version of typical French furnishings of this period. It has cabriole legs and is a delicate, feminine chair.

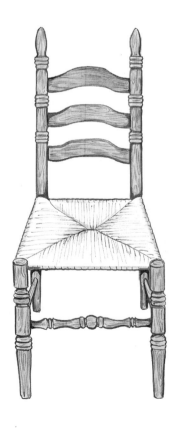

Ladderback

The high back of this Early American chair resembles the rungs of a ladder. Seat can be upholstered, cane, or woven rattan.

Le Corbusier (1887–1965)

Designed by Swiss architect Charles-Edouard Jeanneret, also known as Le Corbusier, this chair has a chrome tubular frame holding square leather cushions. It's very Modern-looking.

Queen Anne (1702–1714)

The most unique feature of Queen Anne chairs are the shapely cabriole legs. The tops of the legs are often carved. The seats of chairs may be upholstered, but the backs are wood. The top of chair can be straight across or have three curved humps. May have claw-and-ball or button feet.

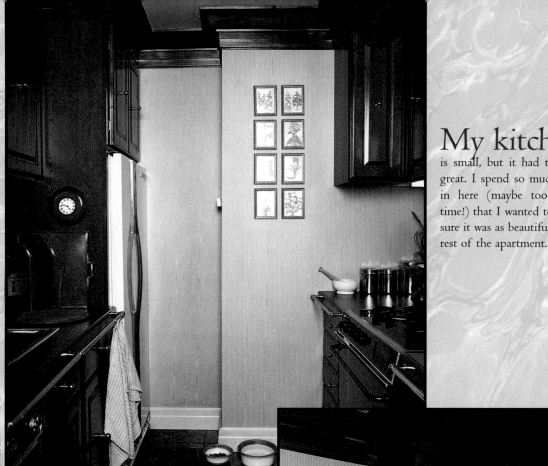

My kitchen

is small, but it had to look great. I spend so much time in here (maybe too much time!) that I wanted to make sure it was as beautiful as the rest of the apartment.

The botanical prints,

thin-striped wallpaper, and dark wood cabinets and molding give the kitchen a real Classic look.

Who would have thought a bathroom could look so Classic? You can't see it in this picture, but I use an Oriental rug instead of one of those fuzzy bathmats. Why not?

We bought the wainscoting at Home Depot and stained it ourselves, and the countertop is a plain piece of wood with a faux-marble finish...I swear!

Frank's office . . . functional yet great-looking. If you have to work, why not do it in style?

Red Chinese

ginger jars, old books, an antique basket, and brass candlesticks make my office an extension of the rest of the house. Groupings...I love them.

My "Wall of Fame."

I thought this was an interesting way to display the awards that mean so much to me and Frank. Yeah, that's it on the left—my Emmy!! We still have to figure out how to play the *Another World* theme song when you step through the door!

Ruffle chair

This is a large, overstuffed chair, always up-holstered or slipcovered. It has a ruffled skirt at the base. Can be used in a Classic room, a Sporty/Country room, or even a Modern one, depending on the fabric.

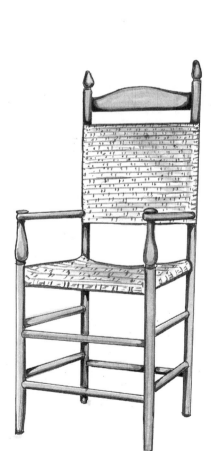

Shaker (19th century)

Made by the Shaker religious sect, this chair has a functional simplicity and austere beauty. Known for its superior crafts-manship, it is unornamented and there are no nails or screws hold-ing the pieces together.

Sheraton (1751–1806)

This is a delicate chair with a rectangular back and legs of fine tapered squares, with upholstered seats. More elaborate versions have carved and gilded arms and legs. (Not pictured.)

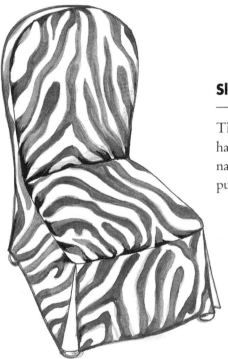

Slipper chair

This is a dainty side or armchair with low legs. It has a round seat and is usually upholstered. Originally designed for use in a bedroom for a lady to put on her slippers.

Stickley (1858–1942)

Gustave Stickley created what is now known as the Mission style of furniture. This chair, made from wood (with a smooth matte finish), has very simple, straight lines. Back and seat could be upholstered. Great for a Sporty/Southwestern room, but could be mixed with any style, depending on the fabric selection.

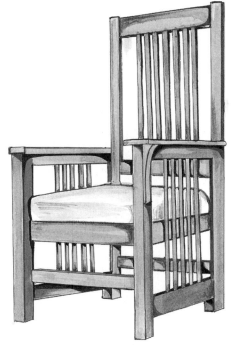

Wicker chair

Originally only used as outdoor furniture, this chair is now becoming more prevalent indoors in dining rooms, living rooms, and bedrooms. Woven from natural fibers, it generally has an upholstered seat or cushion.

Wing chair (1750)

These are large, comfortable, up-holstered (usually overstuffed) chairs with a high back and protruding side pieces, or wings. It was originally designed to keep drafts away from the head. It's an English and Early American style, but with different fabrics, can go with any style.

Windsor (1700)

A chair with a Bentwood back frame and scooped wood seat, with the legs and back rails inserted directly into the seat. The legs can be plain or turned; it can have arms or not.

Sofas

Camelback

This is a design originally made by Hepplewhite, but widely copied. Its main characteristic is the hump along the back, hence the name. While Classic, it can go in any decor, depending on the fabric.

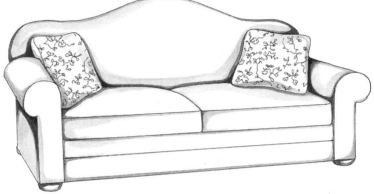

Chaise lounge

This is a chair with a long seat. It differs from a Récamier because the foot end is left open. A chaise lounge can have one or two arms and is in a more traditional style.

Récamier

Chaise lounge with a curved high end. Comes from Empire style, but can be very Modern with the right fabric. (Not pictured.)

Chesterfield

This is an overstuffed sofa with upholstered ends. It usually has short, wood, canister legs. Also seen in leather with deep button tufts. (Not pictured.)

Daybed

This is a twin-size bed that has a headboard, footboard, and a back between the two. It is used as a sofa during the day, with bolsters or pillows along the back, and a bed at night. It is made in every furniture style.

Futon

This is a Japanese-style mattress that can be placed on the floor, on a platform as a bed, or on a frame that folds up to look like a sofa. The frames are made in every furniture style and can be used in any room where you might need an extra bed.

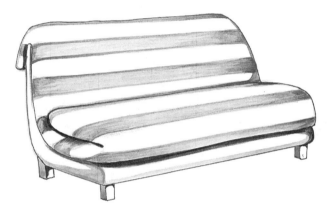

Love seat

A love seat is a small sofa made for two people to sit on. You can find them in styles as diverse as Queen Anne to an Early American wing chair–type.

Sectional

This sofa comes with many pieces that can be moved around to create different shapes. It is also sometimes called a modular sofa (the difference is that a modular usually has only two pieces—a sofa and a love seat that fit together). It is made in many furniture styles from Classic to Modern.

Tuxedo

This is a sofa in which the back and arms are the same height, creating a boxy streamlined look. Can be Modern, but a change of fabric makes it suitable for any style. (Not pictured.)

Tables

Chrome and glass

This style table has chrome legs or a chrome base and might have a chrome border around the top. The center is filled with glass. Can be a dining table, end or coffee table, or a sideboard.

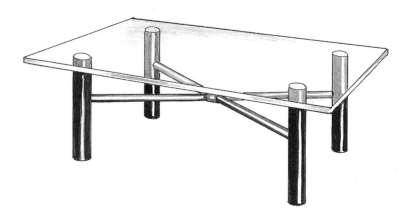

Drop-leaf

This is any table with sides that fold down. They are held up by a small, sliding piece of wood or metal when table is open to full length. Great for small rooms because table can sit against a wall when not in use. (Not pictured.)

Gateleg (17th century)

This table has two drop leaves that are held up by swinging out a "gate" for support. On a true gateleg table, the gate has two upright pieces and at least one horizontal stretcher; tables without the stretchers are called "swing leg" tables.

Hepplewhite (1760–1786)

A Hepplewhite table may have intricate wood inlays and uniquely shaped tops. The legs may be simple squares that taper down to a point at the floor, or they may be turned, but still delicate and fairly simple. (Not pictured.)

Parsons (1965–1970)

This is a square- or rectangular-shaped table with square, unadorned legs that are of the same thickness as the top. It can be made of wood, lacquered, painted, decorative painted, or chrome with a glass top.

Queen Anne (1702–1714)

This table is almost always made in walnut and has the same curved cabriole legs as Queen Anne chairs. The legs are at the four corners, but the table can be round, rectangular, or triangular, too.

Regency (1793–1820)

This table, usually made of mahogany or rosewood, has a top that sits on a single or double pedestal. Four legs come out from each pedestal; there is also usually a brass toe on each leg.

Round pedestal

This is a round table (becomes oval when leaves are inserted to lengthen) that is held up by a single pedestal. Can be wood, laminate, chrome. Also comes in smaller sizes to use as end tables.

Shaker (19th century)

Made by Shaker religious sect, this table has clean lines—a thin top, straight-turned legs. Known for its superior craftsmanship, it is unornamented and there are no nails or screws holding pieces together. Always the utilitarians, Shakers often built a drawer under the table to hold linens or silver.

Beds

Canopy

An earlier style of four-poster bed that has a fabric top. Top is often curved upward to make it look more like a tent. Depending on the design, the material the bed is made from, and the fabric of the canopy, this bed can go in any style room.

Country oak

The headboard, footboard, and side slats are made from natural oak. The wood can be plain or it can have carvings in it. The top can be straight or curved. An oak bed can also have a very tall headboard. This bed is very Country.

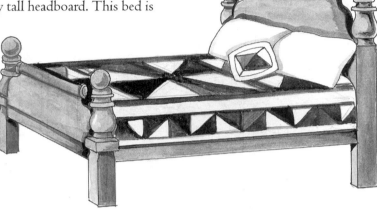

Four-poster

This is a bed with four tall posts, one on each corner. It can be wood, brass, wrought iron. It might also have a frame connecting the four posts on which you can drape fabric.

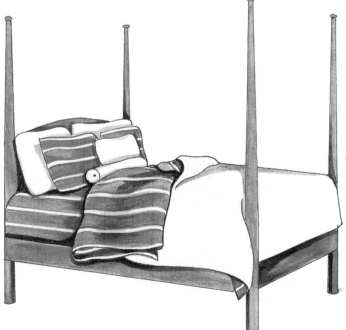

Mission

This bed is heavy and square, mostly made in oak, with obvious joints. It has a rustic quality that suits its beginnings: it was originally built by missionaries and Native Americans. The look was later softened by those like Gustave Stickley.

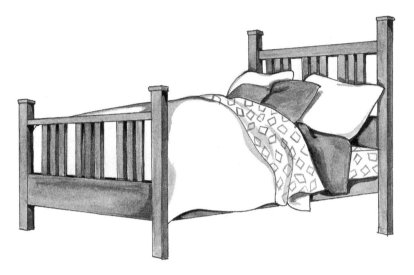

Platform

You can make a platform bed yourself, by building a big square box to hold your mattress (a box spring is not needed). You can use furniture-quality wood or use plywood and paint it, cover it with fabric for a Romantic or Classic room (white damask, with white linens—to die for), cover it with black vinyl for a Modern room, glue on raised panels for an Elegant room.

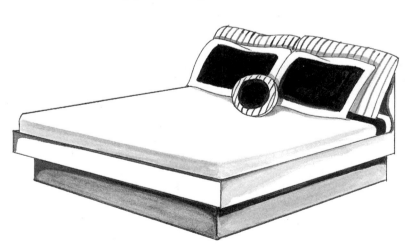

The frame has a scrolled head and footboard. The sleigh bed comes from the American Empire style, and of course, it looks like a sleigh. You can do a daybed look with it by putting lots of pillows along the back. This bed works in any style room and is especially charming in a child's room.

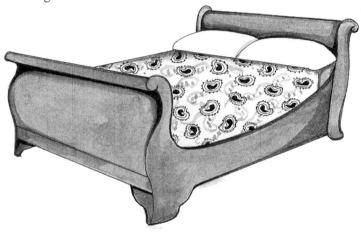

Wrought iron

Headboard and footboard are made from wrought iron. The style can be Modern and very angular, or it can be Country or Romantic, with intricate swirls and flowers. A wrought-iron bed can also be a four-poster.

Lighting

Brass light chandelier

This comes in many of the same shapes as a wrought-iron chandelier but is made in brass. It has anywhere from four to twelve lights. You can use it in any style house, in either a dining room or an entry hall.

Candlestick lamp

This kind of lamp looks like a tall, thin candlestick with a small bulb at the top. It can be made from brass, wood, copper, or glass. You can leave the bulb bare, as I do in my Connecticut home, or you can cover it with a petite shade. Works well in a Classic room with a fabric shade, a Romantic room with a parchment or lace shade, or a Country room with a raffia shade.

Ceiling fan

Ceiling fans move air in a room to make it more comfortable, but they can also have light fixtures attached to the center. The light can be a single globe or three to four individual fixtures to spread light further. The fixtures can be glass, wood, or painted enamel. Use ceiling fans in any room, but especially in the bedrooms. They work in every style home. Remember to have separate switches installed for the fan and the light; you may not want both at once.

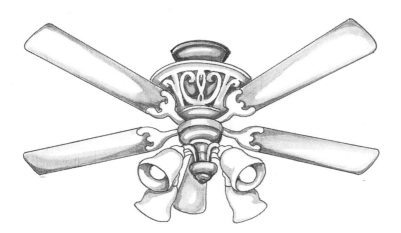

Classic ginger jar in Oriental porcelain

Originally a jar in which to keep ginger, decorators have turned the design into a lamp. Comes mostly in subdued colors and quiet patterns. Shade will usually be in a solid color.

Classic standing lamp

This lamp stands on the floor and comes in a wide variety of finishes. The base can be brass, wood, wrought iron, wicker. It can have a small table attached near the middle. The shade can be brass, fabric, parchment, glass. It provides great light and takes up little space.

Crystal chandelier

This is a large light fixture that belongs in a large room. It is usually made of brass with glass crystals hanging down—the glass can be Austrian, cut glass, colored glass—and hung over a very ornate dining-room table. Really only works in a Classic or an Elegant room. It has a great presence and beautiful light because the light reflects off the crystals.

Flexible table lamp

This is a functional lamp that is task-driven. Put it on a desk where you work, on a table next to where you read, next to a sewing machine. They are portable and can be moved easily as your tasks change. Can be used in any style home.

Hanson lamp

This is a swing-arm lamp that attaches to the wall. It comes in brass, chrome, or enamel (in every color). It's best for task lighting, like reading. Great over a bed.

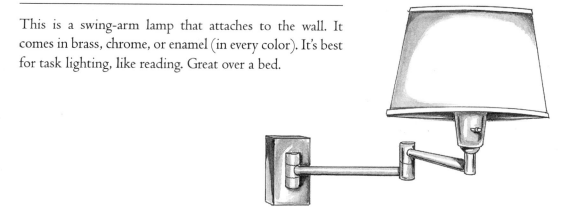

Hurricane lamp

This is a light fixture that is enclosed in a curved, clear-glass case. Antique hurricane lamps use candles instead of bulbs. It can sit on a table or can hang on a wall as a sconce. Depending on the design (square and stark for a Modern look, curvy and delicate for Classic), it can work in any style room.

Italian tizio lamp

This is a Classic-style lamp that is task-driven. Use it for reading, working, sewing. It is usually in brass or chrome and can be used in a Classic, Modern, or Eclectic room.

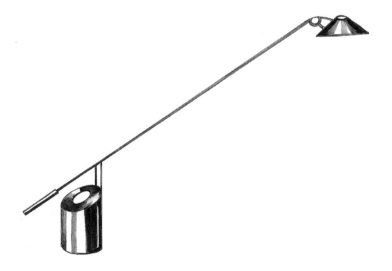

Pendant lamp

This fixture hangs from either a chain or a stem and can have one light fixture or a bar that holds two or three fixtures. You often see them over a pool table, but they can also be used over a desk, in a bathroom, over a long rectangular table, anywhere you need downward-facing light.

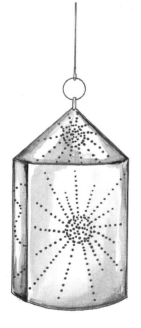

Pierced tin

This is a lamp made from a cylinder (or square) of tin, pierced to create a pattern that releases a soft light. Can sit on a table or hang on a wall. I have one in my hallway in Connecticut because it suits the period of the house (the design is based on a version of Paul Revere's light).

Pottery lamp with pleated shade

Made from earthenware, redware, or glazed porcelain, and topped with a pleated shade. Base can be any color or texture. Shade may be made in linen, silk, or cotton. It could be plain, print, or even plaid, depending on the personality of your room.

Standing torchere

Also called an uplighter, this kind of lamp is designed to provide a mood rather than direct task lighting. It has a triangular-shaped bowl at the top, directing light up. You can use a torchere in a Modern room, a Romantic room, even a Classic room if the lines are simple enough.

Track lighting

Track lighting is any number of light fixtures attached to an electrified track, which is attached to a wall or ceiling. Each fixture can be moved and directed where you need light most. Can be used in any room in any style home.

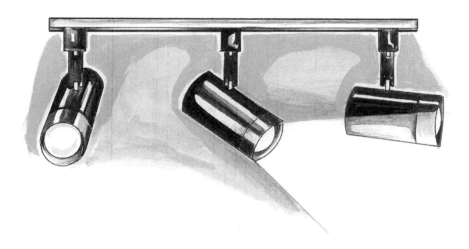

Wall sconce

These are available in many, many styles and are therefore useful in any style home. You might hang them in a hallway, in pairs to frame a mirror, next to your bed. They can be glass enclosed or have fabric shades. They can be antiques that are not electrified and hold candles. So many varieties.

Wrought-iron chandelier with candles

This is a light fixture from another time, perhaps the eighteenth century. Then it was filled with real candles, but this kind of chandelier has been electrified for modern use. It's great in a Country, Romantic, or Southwestern room. Painted a bright red or blue or shiny black, it would be fantastic in a Modern home. You would generally use it over a dining-room table, but you could also hang a small chandelier over a round table at the end of a living-room couch.

Fabric

Brocade

A Jacquard-weave fabric with a raised design woven in. Brocade is a fairly heavy, durable fabric. For: Slipcovers, upholstery, drapes.

Cotton

A natural-fiber fabric that is printed in millions of different designs and finishes. May be matte or shiny. For: Curtains, tablecloths, lamp shade covering. In most cases, cotton fabric is too fragile for slipcovers or upholstery.

Damask

A Jacquard-weave fabric with a pattern woven right into the fabric rather than printed. Pattern reverses on the opposite side. Damask is a durable fabric. For: Slipcovers, upholstery, drapes.

Denim

A twill fabric usually made in blues, but can be any color. For: Heavier weights can be used for slipcovers and upholstery; lighter weights for curtains or table throws.

Embossed acetate

This is a synthetic fabric with a pattern set in with heated rollers to give the look of brocade for a lower cost. For: Slipcovers, drapes, and if sturdy enough, upholstery.

Jacquard

The name of a weave in which you can see the threads. Jacquard-weave fabrics include brocade, damask, and tapestry. For: Depending on weight, slipcovers, upholstery, drapes.

Leather

Real or synthetic leather is available in many colors, even previously unheard of reds and blues. For: Upholstery. Great for family-room sofas; wears and cleans well.

Muslin

Plain-weave fabric made in many weights, from very, very thin to course and heavy. Usually made in off-white and other muted tones. Can be made in a Jacquard weave. For: Depending on weight, muslin can be used for just about anything. It is very durable and washable. Often used for curtain linings.

Tapestry

This is a heavy multicolored fabric, usually with a picture woven into the design. Can be made from silk, wool, cotton, or a blend. For: Drapes, upholstery, slip-covers, pillows.

Toile de Jouy

Floral or scenic design printed on fabric, often reproductions of well-known paintings. For: Drapes, chair-seat covers, lamp shade covering, pillows.

Tweed

A heavy-weight twill fabric made with a rough-textured wool yarn. For: Upholstery.

Twill

A name for fabrics made with a diagonal wale on the face. Fabrics include tweed, denim, and gabardine. For: Slipcovers, upholstery.

Velvet

A fabric with an extra yarn woven in, which is then cut and brushed to create a soft surface. Can also have a pattern woven in Jacquard style. For: Drapes, table throws, pillows. Heavier weights can be used for slipcovers.

Final Note

O kay, you've done it. . . .

You've redesigned your home to reflect the real you. You walk in and feel a calm settle over your entire body and soul. If you've followed me all the way through Finding Your Style, the Basics, Painting, Lighting, etc., I know you've worked hard. It's not easy translating the style you envision in your head into real-live rooms that work. So, pat yourself on the back and bring a tray filled with champagne and hors d'oeuvres into your newly redecorated living room. Put your feet up and enjoy the view. I can't wait to visit.